TIMELINES OF HISTORY

VOLUME 6

A WIDER WORLD

1500–1600

GROLIER

an imprint of

SCHOLASTIC

www.scholastic.com/librarypublishing

Published by Grolier,
an imprint of Scholastic Library Publishing,
Sherman Turnpike
Danbury, Connecticut 06816

© 2005 The Brown Reference Group plc

Set ISBN 0-7172-6002-X
Volume 6 ISBN 0-7172-6008-9

Library of Congress Cataloging-in-Publication Data

Timelines of history.
        p. cm.
    Includes index.
    Contents: v. 1. The early empires, prehistory—500 B.C. —
v. 2. The classical age, 500 B.C.—500 A.D. — v. 3. Raiders and
conquerors, 500—1000 — v. 4. The feudal era, 1000—1250 —
v. 5. The end of the Middle Ages, 1250—1500 — v. 6. A wider
world, 1500—1600 — v. 7. Royalty and revolt, 1600—1700 —
v. 8. The Age of Reason, 1700—1800 — v. 9. Industry and
empire, 1800—1900 — v. 10. The modern world, 1900—2000.
    ISBN 0-7172-6002-X (set : alk. paper) — ISBN 0-7172-
6003-8 (v. 1 : alk. paper) — ISBN 0-7172-6004-6 (v. 2 : alk.
paper) — ISBN 0-7172-6005-4 (v. 3 : alk. paper) — ISBN 0-
7172-6006-2 (v. 4 : alk. paper) — ISBN 0-7172-6007-0 (v. 5 :
alk. paper) — ISBN 0-7172-6008-9 (v. 6 : alk. paper) — ISBN
0-7172-6009-7 (v. 7 : alk. paper) — ISBN 0-7172-6010-0 (v. 8
: alk.paper) — ISBN 0-7172-6011-9 (v. 9 : alk. paper) —
ISBN 0-7172-6012-7 (v. 10 : alk. paper)
    1. Chronology, Historical

For information address the publisher:
Grolier, Sherman Turnpike,
Danbury, Connecticut 06816

Printed and bound in Thailand

FOR THE BROWN REFERENCE GROUP PLC

Consultant: Professor Jeremy Black, University of Exeter

Project Editor: Tony Allan
Designers: Frankie Wood
Picture Researcher: Sharon Southren
Cartographic Editor: Tim Williams
Design Manager: Lynne Ross
Production: Alastair Gourlay, Maggie Copeland
Senior Managing Editor: Tim Cooke
Editorial Director: Lindsey Lowe
Writers: Susan Kennedy, Michael Kerrigan, Peter Lewis

PICTURE CREDITS
(t = top, b = bottom, c = center, l = left, r = right)

Cover
Corbis: Christie's Images b.

AKG-images: 9b, 14t, 21b, 23t, 32, 33t, 40t, 42l, Eric Lessing 45,
Jean-Louis Nou 6b, Rabatti-Dominigie 13l; **The Art Archive:**
38b, Bodleian Library, Oxford 19b; **Bridgeman.co.uk:** Christie's
Images, London 14b, Biblioteca Estense, Modena, Italy 8,
Giraudon 23b, Giraudon/Topkapi Palace Museum, Istanbul,
Turkey 28r, Johnny van Haeften Gallery, London 43b,
Hermitage, St. Petersburg, Russia 34b, Museum of Fine Arts,
Houston, Texas, USA 34t, Victoria & Albert Museum, London
18b; **Corbis:** Archivo Iconografico, S.A. 43t, James L. Amos 25b,
Arte Immagini srl 18c, Stefano Bianchetti 22, Burnstein
Collection 10t, Christie's Images, London 15, Raymond Gehman
38t, Gianni Giansanti/Immaginazione 7, Chris Hellier 29t,
Historical Picture Archive 44t, H.H. Huey 16t, John Heseltine
21t, The Mariner's Museum 39t, Frances G.Mayer 26t, Gianni
Dagli Orti 10b, 20, David Reed 12b, Stapleton Collection 6t,
Brian A.Vikander 30b, Roger Wood 42r; **Sylvia Cordaiy Photo
Library:** Geoffrey Taunton 36b; **Peter Langer, Associated Media
Group:** 26b; **Photos.com:** 40cr; **Photos12.com:** ARJ 16b, 18-19t,
Oasis 17t, 25t, 30t, 39b; **Skyscan:** 44-45b; **TopFoto.co.uk:** 31, 34-
35c, 35b, 36t, HIP 28l, 40b, /The British Library 27, /Ann Ronan
Picture Library 24l; **Travel Ink:** David Toase 33b; **Werner
Forman Archive:** 11, 12t.

The Brown Reference Group has made every effort to trace
copyright holders of the pictures used in this book. Anyone
having claims to ownership not identified above is invited to
contact The Brown Reference Group.

CONTENTS

HOW TO USE THIS BOOK

INTRODUCTION

This volume covers the first century of common global history that marked the beginning of the modern era. European contact with the Americas quickly brought about the collapse of the Aztec and Inca empires. Spanish conquistadors shipped back quantities of gold and silver to Europe, while Portuguese ships dominated a flourishing spice trade in the Indian Ocean. But China was still the world's greatest trading power, exporting cotton, silk, and tea to Southeast Asia and then on to Europe, newly rich thanks to its American silver.

Meanwhile Europe underwent cultural and religious upheavals as the ideas of the Renaissance spread, and the Protestant Reformation split the church. After bitter wars of religion in Germany, France, and the Netherlands, by 1600 almost 40 percent of the continent's population was Protestant, although southern and eastern Europe remained predominantly Catholic. The Ottoman Empire successfully challenged Spain for control of the North African coast and pushed its frontiers farther into southeast Europe; it also became a major West Asia power after conquering Iraq from the Safavid Empire of Persia.

Farther east the Mughals, a Central Asian dynasty, conquered northern India and created a prosperous Muslim empire. Russia nearly doubled in size as it conquered Central Asia, bringing its southern frontier to the Caspian Sea, and expanded east into Siberia. At the end of the century European influence had spread around the coasts of Africa as Portugal established a string of fortified ports to dominate trade. Kanem-Bornu, on the southern edge of the Sahara Desert, was the leading Islamic state in Africa, while Great Zimbabwe, once the capital of an extensive southern empire, was in decline.

ABBREVIATIONS	
mi	miles
cm	centimeters
m	meters
km	kilometers
sq. km	square kilometers
mya	million years ago
c.	about (from the Latin word circa)

A NOTE ON DATES

This set follows standard Western practice in dating events from the start of the Christian era, presumed to have begun in the year 0. Those that happened before the year 0 are listed as B.C. (before the Christian era), and those that happened after as A.D. (from the Latin Anno Domini, meaning "in the year of the Lord"). Wherever possible, exact dates are given; where there is uncertainty, the date is prefixed by the abbreviation c. (short for Latin circa, meaning "about") to show that it is approximate.

ABOUT THIS SET

This book is one of a set of ten providing timelines for world history from the beginning of recorded history up to 2000 A.D. Each volume arranges events that happened around the world within a particular period and is made up of three different types of facing two-page spreads: timelines, features, and glossary pages ("Facts at a Glance," at the back of the book). The three should be used in combination to find the information that you need. Timelines list events that occurred between the dates shown on the pages and cover periods ranging from several centuries at the start of Volume 1, dealing with early times, to six or seven years in Volumes 9 and 10, addressing the modern era.

In part, the difference reflects the fact that much more is known about recent times than about distant eras. Yet it also reflects a real acceleration in the number of noteworthy events, related to surging population growth. Demographers estimate that it was only in the early 19th century that world population reached one billion; at the start of the 21st century the figure is over six billion and rising, meaning that more people have lived in the past 200 years than in all the other epochs of history combined.

The subjects covered by the feature pages may be a major individual or a civilization. Some cover epoch-making events, while others address more general themes such as the development of types of technology. In each case the feature provides a clear overview of its subject to supplement its timeline entries, indicating its significance on the broader canvas of world history.

Facts at a Glance lists names and terms that may be unfamiliar or that deserve more explanation than can be provided in the timeline entries. Check these pages for quick reference on individuals, peoples, battles, or cultures, and also for explanations of words that are not clear.

The comprehensive index at the back of each book covers the entire set and will enable you to follow all references to a given subject across the ten volumes.

TIMELINE PAGES

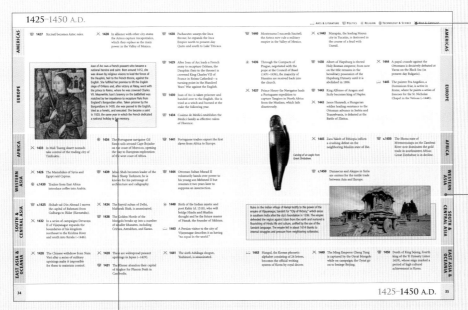

Symbols
Each entry is prefixed by one of five symbols—for example, crossed swords for war, an open book for arts and literature—indicating a particular category of history. A key to the symbols is printed at the top of the right-hand page.

Bands
Each timeline is divided into five or six bands relating to different continents or other major regions of the world. Within each band events are listed in chronological (time) order.

Boxes
Boxes in each timeline present more detailed information about important individuals, places, events, or works.

FEATURE PAGES

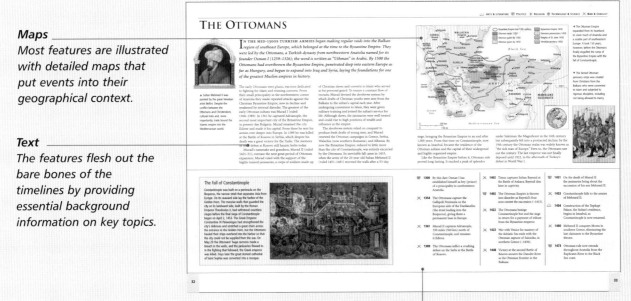

Maps
Most features are illustrated with detailed maps that put events into their geographical context.

Text
The features flesh out the bare bones of the timelines by providing essential background information on key topics.

Subject-specific timelines
Each feature has a timeline devoted exclusively to its topic to give an at-a-glance overview of the main developments in its history.

1500–1510 A.D.

AMERICAS

👑 **c.1500** The Inca Empire in Peru reaches its high point under Huayna Capac (r.1493–1525).

⚙ **1500** The Portuguese navigator Gaspar de Côrte-Real makes the first authenticated landfall on the North American mainland since Vikings explored Labrador five centuries previously.

👑 **1500** The Portuguese explorer Pedro Álvarez Cabral claims Brazil for Portugal under the terms of the Treaty of Tordesillas.

⚙ **1501** The colonial plantation system is initiated when Spain transfers sugarcane cultivation from Madeira to Hispaniola.

EUROPE

⚙ **c.1500** In Siegershausen, Switzerland, Jakob Nufer performs the first recorded caesarean birth operation on a living woman.

⚔ **1500** French forces under Louis XII overrun and annex the Duchy of Milan. The Treaty of Granada partitions Italy between France and Spain

⚔ **1501** Russia begins its expansion as Czar Ivan III invades Poland–Lithuania.

⚙ **1503** The Spanish office of American trade ("Casa de Contratación") is set up in Seville.

☀ **1503** Julius II becomes pope; a patron of the arts, he commissions the rebuilding of St. Peter's Cathedral by Bramante and the painting of the Sistine Chapel ceiling by Michelangelo (–1512)

👑 **1504** Death of Isabella I of Castile; Ferdinand II ("the Catholic") of Aragon rules Castile as regent in place of Isabella's mentally ill daughter Juana.

⚙ **c.1505** In Nuremberg, Germany, the clockmaker Peter Henlein introduces a timepiece driven by springs rather than weights, enabling the invention of portable watches

📖 **1506** Leonardo da Vinci paints the *Mona Lisa* and compiles his notebooks on mechanics, anatomy, and astronomy (–1509).

📖 **1507** German cartographer Martin Waldseemüller publishes *Cosmographiae Introductio*, a map on which the name "America" is first used.

AFRICA

⚔ **1504** In Sudan, the Muslim Funj defeat the Christian rulers of Sennar between the Blue and White Niles.

⚔ **1505** Kilwa on the East African coast is sacked by Francisco de Almeida's Portuguese troops.

👑 **1508** Lebna Denegel becomes emperor of Ethiopia and struggles against growing Islamic influence.

WESTERN ASIA

👑 **1501** Shah Esmail overthrows the "White Sheep" Turkmen rulers of Persia and founds the Safavid Dynasty.

⚔ **1502** Tatars destroy the last remnants of the Mongol Golden Horde, opening the way for Russian expansion into the Caucasus.

SOUTH & CENTRAL ASIA

👑 **c.1500** Muslim khanates emerge centered on the oasis cities of the Silk Road to the West.

Babur, founder of India's Mughal Dynasty, watches a wrestling match.

⚙ **1500** Pedro Álvarez Cabral lands at Cochin and Cannonore, establishing trade links between Portugal and India.

EAST ASIA & OCEANIA

👑 **c.1500** The Hindu–Buddhist kingdom of Majapahit is weakened by the spread of Islam to Borneo and Java.

⚙ **c.1500** The Chinese inventor Wan Hu is killed trying to pilot a flying machine made of a chair, two kites, and 47 rockets.

AMERICAS

1502 Amerigo Vespucci ventures down the east coast of South America.

1502 Montezuma II becomes the last Aztec Emperor of Mexico; during his reign (to 1520) the empire reaches its zenith.

1505 The first African slaves arrive in the Americas, at Santo Domingo, starting the transatlantic slave trade.

1508 The Spanish expand their territory in the Caribbean and Central America with the conquest of Puerto Rico (–1511).

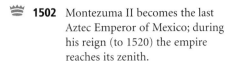

A fanciful 16th-century engraving by Theodor de Bry shows the Italian explorer Amerigo Vespucci arriving in Bermuda.

EUROPE

1508 The League of Cambrai is formed by Aragon, France, Spain, and the Holy Roman Empire against Venice.

1509 Henry VIII ascends the throne in England and marries his first wife, Catharine of Aragon.

One of the greatest showplaces of the art of the Italian Renaissance, the Sistine Chapel in Rome's Vatican Palace was first commissioned by Pope Sixtus IV in the 1470s. Over the following years its walls were decorated with frescoes by some of the finest artists of the day, including Perugino and Botticelli. Its greatest masterpieces, however, were added from 1508 on by Michelangelo. Despite bitter quarrels with Pope Julius II, his patron, he spent four years working in uncomfortable conditions covering the building's ceiling in paintings. Twenty-five years later he was summoned back by a new pope to decorate the west wall behind the altar and produced another great work, *The Last Judgment*.

AFRICA

1508 The Portuguese establish Mozambique as their first colony in Africa.

1509 Spain captures Oran in Algeria, beginning a campaign to take key bases on the North African coast.

WESTERN ASIA

1503 The war setting Venice and Hungary against the Ottoman Empire comes to an end.

1504 Venice sends an envoy to the Ottoman Sultan Bayezid II proposing the construction of a Suez Canal.

1509 The Ottoman capital Istanbul is rocked by a devastating earthquake that kills 10,000 people.

SOUTH & CENTRAL ASIA

1504 In Afghanistan Mughal forces under Babur begin a series of conquests that will eventually establish their rule over the whole Indian subcontinent.

1509 Krishnadevaraya, newly appointed king of the Hindu state of Vijayanagar, repels an attack by Sultan Mahmud of Bidar.

1509 A Portuguese fleet under Francisco de Almeida defeats an Egyptian–Gujarati fleet at Diu, securing control over the spice trade.

EAST ASIA & OCEANIA

1506 In Korea the tyrant Yonsangun is deposed by a rebellion that brings Chungjong to the throne (–1507).

1500–1510 A.D.

IN THE WAKE OF COLUMBUS

DRIVEN BY THE URGE TO CHART *new territories and to explore new commercial opportunities, many intrepid seafarers followed the example of Christopher Columbus and set sail from Europe for distant regions to the west and east with only crude navigational instruments to guide them. The voyages of Magellan, Vespucci, and others opened up lands and oceans previously unknown to Europeans and established new trade routes. By 1600 the ground was laid for the system of international commerce on which all modern economies are based.*

▲ A Portuguese merchant gathers outsize sticks of cinnamon, collected in Sri Lanka, for transport back to Europe. Used as a flavoring, cinnamon was one of the most prized of the spices that spurred the European voyages of exploration; at one time it was said to be more valuable than gold.

Portuguese mariners were at the forefront of exploration in the 16th century. In 1511 Afonso de Albuquerque seized the port of Malacca on the Malaysian peninsula, securing a key center of the East Indian spice trade for Portugal. Venturing out from Goa—a base on India's west coast seized by Albuquerque the previous year—the Portuguese discovered the "Spice Islands" (the Moluccas, now part of Indonesia). Trade with China began in 1520, and by 1557 Portugal had founded a permanent base at Macao, on China's south coast. Farther east Japan's isolation ended with the landing of Portuguese merchants on the small island of Tanegashima in 1542. The supremacy of Portugal's seaborne trading empire in the East went unchallenged until the rise of the Dutch and British East India Companies in the following century.

Portugal's most famous 16th-century explorer, Ferdinand Magellan, was sailing in the service of the Spanish king in 1519 when he traveled to the tip of South America and through the strait that now bears his name. Crossing the Pacific, he pioneered a new westward route from Europe to the East Indies. Although he himself was killed on the Philippine island of Cebu, one of his ships under the command of Sebastian del Cano went on to complete the first circumnavigation of the world in 1522.

Like Columbus, Amerigo Vespucci was an Italian navigator–merchant working for Spain. On his second trip to America, from 1499 to 1500, he sighted the mouth of the mighty Amazon River. On further voyages, this time on Portugal's behalf, he explored the coast of what is now Brazil as far south as the River Plate. Vespucci was one of the first explorers to promote the idea that the New World was not part of the Indies, as Columbus had believed, but a seperate continent, and contemporary mapmakers duly named it "America" in his honor.

⊛ **1500** Portuguese explorers led by Pedro Álvarez Cabral discover Brazil.

⊛ **1507** The German cartographer Martin Waldseemüller names the continent of America in honor of the Florentine navigator Amerigo Vespucci.

✕ **1509** The Portuguese under Francisco de Almeida defeat a combined Indian and Mameluke Egyptian fleet off Diu, Gujarat, so gaining control of the Indian Ocean.

⊛ **1513** A Spanish expedition led by Vasco Nuñez de Balboa crosses the Isthmus of Panama and claims the "South Sea" (Pacific Ocean) for Spain.

⊛ **1519** Fernão de Magalhães (Ferdinand Magellan) sails through the Magellan Strait and discovers the western passage to the East Indies (–1522).

♛ **1522** The Ming Emperor Jia Qing expels the Portuguese from China for piracy.

⊛ **1531** The first international stock exchange opens in Antwerp, becoming the center of European trade and finance until 1576.

♛ **1557** Portugal establishes a permanent trading and missionary settlement at Macao in the Pearl River Delta of southern China.

⊛ **1570** Nagasaki in southern Japan is opened up to foreign trade by the local daimyo (lord) Omura.

✕ **1576** During the Dutch revolt against Spanish rule Antwerp is sacked by unpaid and starving Spanish troops (again in 1585). Its importance as a trading center begins to wane in favor of Amsterdam.

⊛ **1595** The first Dutch maritime expedition to the East Indies marks the beginning of the Dutch overseas trading empire (–1597).

⊛ **1600** Foundation of the English East India Company in India.

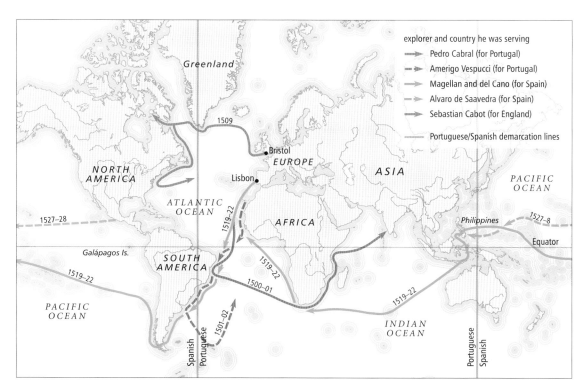

explorer and country he was serving
➤ Pedro Cabral (for Portugal)
➤ Amerigo Vespucci (for Portugal)
➤ Magellan and del Cano (for Spain)
➤ Alvaro de Saavedra (for Spain)
➤ Sebastian Cabot (for England)

— Portuguese/Spanish demarcation lines

◄ The great voyages of exploration of the late 15th and early 16th centuries linked parts of the world that had previously been barely if at all aware of each other's existence. Sailing from Spain, Portugal, and England, brave mariners traveled west to the New World of America and east to India. In 1522 Sebastian del Cano—second in command to Ferdinand Magellan, who had been killed en route—completed the first circumnavigation of the world.

The Spanish were eager to set up colonies to exploit the New World's riches. Alonso de Ojeda, who had sailed with Columbus and Vespucci, claimed large parts of northeastern South America for Spain in 1509. He named Venezuela after seeing native houses built over the water—like those in Venice. Two years later Vasco Nuñez de Balboa founded the settlement of Darien (present-day Panama). Balboa's search for gold took him across the narrow Central American isthmus, and on September 29, 1513, he became the first European to see the Pacific Ocean, finally disproving Columbus's claim to have reached India.

Thus far Spain's American settlements were on a small scale. Soon, however, Hernán Cortés and Francisco Pizarro were to seize control of Mexico and Peru, ushering in the age of the conquistadors.

A Taste for Spices

Spices had been prized in Europe since Roman times as flavorings for food and ingredients in medicines. Grown in tropical regions, they were brought by land to ports in West Asia; from there Venice came to control their import into Europe. The urge to gain direct access to spices drove much of the eastward exploration in the 16th century. Portugal began to ship pepper from India (right), cinnamon from Sri Lanka, nutmeg and cloves from the Moluccas, and ginger from China. Spices were easy to carry in bulk and highly profitable. To cut transport costs to northern Europe, the Portuguese moved their main distribution center from Lisbon to Amsterdam and Antwerp. By 1530 Antwerp was Europe's richest city, and its wealth increased further when it became the hub for Spanish silver imports from Peru.

AMERICAS

✕ **1511** Diego Velazquez leads the Spanish conquest of Cuba, a springboard for further invasions of Central America (–1515).

✱ **1513** A Spanish force under Vasco Nuñez de Balboa crosses the Isthmus of Darien (Panama) and sights the Pacific Ocean.

EUROPE

✕ **1511** The pope forms an alliance (the Holy League) with Venice, Spain, and the Holy Roman emperor to drive the French from Italy; its forces are defeated at the Battle of Ravenna (1512).

👑 **1513** The Union of Kalmar, which has linked Denmark, Norway, and Sweden since 1397, comes under strain as Sweden (then including Finland) breaks away.

👑 **1513** The Italian political theorist Niccolò Macchiavelli writes *The Prince*, a key work on statecraft that instructs rulers on how to hold power.

✱ **1515** The wheel-lock arquebus (early musket) is developed in Germany as a replacement for the unreliable matchlock.

📖 **1516** The English scholar Thomas More publishes *Utopia*, which describes an ideal social and political system.

AFRICA

👑 **1512** The Songhai Empire, ruled by Askia Mohammed, vies for supremacy with the Hausa Confederation in West Africa (–1517).

✱ **1517** Archduke Charles of Austria (later Emperor Charles V) grants a monopoly on the trade in African slaves to merchants from Florence.

✕ **1517** Tuman Bey, the last Mameluke sultan of Egypt, is hanged after an Ottoman army sacks Cairo.

WESTERN ASIA

👑 **1510** Shah Esmail I of Persia drives the Uzbeks out of the disputed region of Khurasan; he has the skull of their leader Mohammed Shaibani made into a drinking cup. In the same year he makes the Shiite branch of Islam the state religion of Persia.

👑 **1511** Selim I ("the Grim") deposes his father Bayezid II to become Ottoman sultan and orders the death of 40,000 Shiite Muslims (–1512); in his nine-year reign the empire will double in size.

✕ **1514** At the Battle of Chaldiran Selim's Ottoman forces defeat Shah Esmail's Persians; the Ottoman Empire expands south and east.

SOUTH & CENTRAL ASIA

⚙ **1510** Afonso de Albuquerque establishes Goa as a Portuguese colony on the west coast of India.

☀ **1514** Under Khan Sayid of Kashgar the Taklamakan Desert region falls under the sway of Islam.

👑 **1518** Portugal signs a peace treaty with Kotte, a kingdom on Sri Lanka.

✕ **1519** Led by Babur, the Mughals undertake the first of many invasions of India.

EAST ASIA & OCEANIA

✕ **1510** Japanese pirates repeatedly pillage the coastal settlements of southern China.

✱ **1511** Portuguese forces seize Malacca on the Malay Peninsula, center of the East Indies spice trade.

A Portuguese merchant trades in nutmegs, along with mace and cloves one of the main exports of the Moluccas or Spice Islands (now part of Indonesia). The Portuguese monopoly on trade with the islands was first challenged by the Dutch at the start of the 17th century.

AMERICAS

⊛ **1513**   The conquistador Juan Ponce de León discovers and names Florida, claiming the territory for Spain.

⊛ **1517**   The Spanish explorer Francisco de Córdoba discovers the Mayan civilization on the Yucatán Peninsula in Central America.

✕ **1519**   An expeditionary force led by the conquistador Hernán Cortés sets out from Cuba to conquer the Aztec Empire of Mexico.

EUROPE

Charles V was the mightiest European ruler of his day. He owed his powers to the marriage alliances of his Hapsburg forebears, which led him to inherit the Netherlands in 1506 and the throne of Spain in 1516. In 1519 he was crowned Holy Roman emperor. He spent his long reign enmeshed in struggles with France, his main rival on the continent, and fighting to defend the Catholic church against the rise of Protestantism. Exhausted by the task, he abdicated all his powers in 1556 and spent the last two years of his life in a monastery.

👑 **1516**   In Venice Jews are forced to live in a separate, walled area of the city—the world's first ghetto.

☀ **1517**   Martin Luther publishes his *95 Theses* in Wittenberg, Germany, detailing abuses by the Catholic church and starting the Reformation.

☀ **1518**   Ulrich Zwingli promotes the Reformation in Switzerland, persuading Zurich city council to ban the sale of indulgences by Catholic monks.

👑 **1519**   Spain's Hapsburg King Charles I is chosen as Holy Roman Emperor Charles V, linking Spain and its colonies with Burgundy and the German lands in a single empire.

⊛ **1519**   The Portuguese navigator Ferdinand Magellan leaves Spain with five ships to find a western route to the Spice Islands; one of his ships will eventually circumnavigate the world (–1522).

AFRICA

👑 **1518**   The Barbary states of Tunis and Algiers are established on the North African coast; they will become notorious bases for raids on Mediterranean shipping.

⊛ **1518**   The transatlantic slave trade gears up as the Spanish authorities grant a license permitting 4,000 African slaves to be imported into the New World.

WESTERN ASIA

⊛ **1515**   The Portuguese viceroy Afonso de Albuquerque takes Hormuz at the mouth of the Persian Gulf.

👑 **1517**   Mecca comes under Ottoman rule when the city's ruler surrenders to Selim.

This Ottoman pulpit tile bears a plan of the Muslim holy city of Mecca. The Kaaba, a square shrine, can be seen in the center.

SOUTH & CENTRAL ASIA

☀ **1519**   Guru Nanak founds the Sikh religion at Kartarpur in the Punjab region of India.

EAST ASIA & OCEANIA

⊛ **1513**   The first Portuguese ships reach the Moluccas, the fabled "Spice Islands"; Portugal enjoys a monopoly on the nutmeg and mace trade for almost a century.

👑 **1514**   Ali Mughayat Syah becomes the first sultan of Aceh in western Sumatra, a rising power in Southeast Asia.

⊛ **1517**   Portuguese sailors discover Taiwan off the Chinese coast, naming it Ilha Formosa ("beautiful island").

1510–1520 A.D.

GREAT ZIMBABWE

▲ An ivory carving shows one of the Portuguese merchants who eventually took over Africa's east coast trade.

*F*ROM AROUND 1000 A.D. *several small chiefdoms rose and fell between the Zambezi and Limpopo rivers in southern Africa. By 1300 the royal center of Great Zimbabwe on the Zambezian plateau (covering the eastern part of the modern state of Zimbabwe) had come to dominate the whole region. Yet by the end of the 16th century even this great city-state had been eclipsed and was in decline.*

The Karanaga, a Shona-speaking people, built the palace-city of Great Zimbabwe between the 12th and 15th centuries. Apart from its sheer size—the site covered a huge area of 1,800 acres (7 sq. km)—its most striking feature was its stone architecture (the word *zimbabwe* comes from a term meaning "sacred houses of rock"). The city was by far the largest complex of stone buildings in sub-Saharan Africa, and many of its massive walls have survived into modern times. Like builders in the Inca Empire in South America, the masons who made Great Zimbabwe hewed blocks of granite and fit them together perfectly, using no mortar. The walls were then carved with intricate herringbone and zigzag patterns.

Because its builders had no written language and so left behind no records of their history, many mysteries surround the rise, zenith, and fall of the complex. At its peak in around 1400 it was probably home to some 20,000 people, most of whom lived in mud huts that have long since disappeared. The wide, grassy plains that surrounded the site were ideal for grazing the cattle that were a vital element of the kingdom's economy. But herding alone could not sustain the population, and the soil was too thin to support intensive agriculture.

Instead, many inhabitants are thought to have lived from trade. Their commerce was based on the rich gold deposits on the Zambezian Plateau, for Great Zimbabwe was strategically placed to control the supply of the mineral to Arab and Swahili traders. Its merchants transported the gold and ivory—another key trade commodity—to the port of Sofala, 280 miles (450 km) away on Africa's east coast. There the goods were exchanged for cotton cloth and other imports. The discovery of Chinese Ming pottery in Zimbabwe bears witness to such transactions.

The Great Enclosure

Of all the puzzles posed by Great Zimbabwe, the Great Enclosure is the most enigmatic. The most striking of the city's stone remains, this compound (also known as the Elliptical Building) has walls 32 feet (10 m) high and up to 17 feet (over 5 m) thick. Parts of the structure may have been plastered with a substance called *daga*, a mixture of decomposed granite and gravel. The fortifications clearly were built for defense, but archeologists disagree about what they were intended to protect. Some think that the enclosure, whose remains include a solid conical tower 30 feet (9 m) high (left), was designed as a place for the city's rulers to smelt gold. Others see it as a home for either the ruler himself or his principal wife, or as a sacred precinct reserved for religious worship.

Whatever its purpose, the Great Enclosure still dominates the site of Great Zimbabwe. Its remains so impressed the first European visitors to the site that they were convinced the city was the capital of the biblical Queen of Sheba.

◀ For centuries Great Zimbabwe was unknown territory to Europeans until it was rediscovered in 1867. This Italian map of the Congo lands to the northwest dates to 1575.

▼ The lands ruled from Great Zimbabwe covered a wide area of what is now the eastern part of the state of Zimbabwe. Graves from the 14th century have been found at Ingombe Ilede, 300 miles (500 km) to the north.

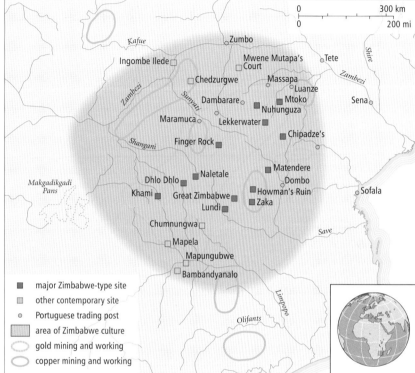

major Zimbabwe-type site
other contemporary site
Portuguese trading post
area of Zimbabwe culture
gold mining and working
copper mining and working

From around 1450 on, however, a new force emerged to challenge Great Zimbabwe's preeminence in the region. The gold-producing provinces rose up, taking control of most of the plateau region in their own name. They were led by Chief Mutota, who came to be known as Mwene Mutapa ("Lord of the Plundered Lands"), a name that came to be applied not just to his successors but also to the kingdom itself, which, weakened by rebellion, fell into decline in the early 17th century.

👑 **c.1200** The Shona-speaking Karanga people first rise to prominence in the Great Zimbabwe area.

👑 **c.1400** Great Zimbabwe is at its peak, grown rich by trading gold to the coast.

⊕ **c.1400** Swahili settlements thrive on the East African coast, trading in gold, ivory, iron, and slaves with Arabs from Zanzibar and elsewhere.

👑 **c.1400** The Zulu and Xhosa peoples establish kingdoms in southern Africa.

👑 **c.1450** Great Zimbabwe goes into decline as Mwene Mutapa rises.

☀ **1490** The Portuguese convert Nzinga Nkuwu, ruler of the Kingdom of Kongo, to Christianity. Mbanza Kongo, its capital, has 30,000 inhabitants when the Europeans arrive.

⊕ **1505** The Portuguese establish a trading post at Sofala on Africa's eastern seaboard (in present-day Mozambique).

👑 **c.1550** Mwene Mutapa is at the height of its power; lying between the Zambezi and Limpopo rivers, its sphere of influence extends from the Kalahari Desert in the west to the Indian Ocean in the east.

⊕ **1570** Portugal establishes a colony in Angola, southwest Africa, as a major center of the transatlantic slave trade.

👑 **c.1600** By this date the Rozwi Empire is dominant in the region once controlled by Great Zimbabwe.

✕ **c.1610** Gatsi Rusere, ruler of Mwene Mutapa, cedes the mineral wealth of his kingdom in return for Portuguese help in putting down a rebellion.

👑 **1652** The Dutch establish a first colony at the Cape of Good Hope. Farmers ("Boers") forcibly take land from the native San and Khoikhoi peoples.

1520–1530 A.D.

AMERICAS

✕ **1520** A popular uprising forces the Spanish conquistadors led by Hernán Cortés to flee the Aztec capital of Tenochtitlán.

⚙ **1520** The Portuguese navigator Ferdinand Magellan passes through the straits at America's southermost tip, later named after him.

✕ **1521** Cortés returns to capture Tenochtitlán, making the Spanish masters of the Aztec Empire.

EUROPE

✕ **1520** Christian II of Denmark and Norway defeats the Swedes at Lake Asunden and massacres their leaders in the Stockholm Bloodbath.

👑 **1520** Charles V is crowned Holy Roman emperor at Aachen.

✕ **1521** War breaks out in Italy between the French occupying Milan and the forces of Charles V and the papacy.

☀ **1521** The Diet of Worms declares Martin Luther to be a heretic.

☀ **1520** Martin Luther is excommunicated and declared a heretic.

✕ **1521** Belgrade falls to the Ottoman Turks.

Stirred into action by the ferment of the Reformation, farm workers across southern Germany took up arms against their landlords in the Peasants' War of 1524 to 1526. Although their grievances were mainly economic, many of the rebels also took up the Protestant cause, much to the horror of Martin Luther, who wrote a pamphlet *Against the Murdering, Thieving Hordes of Peasants*. The revolt was put down with much brutality; in all, 100,000 peasants were killed.

AFRICA

☀ **1520** The Portuguese priest Francisco Alvarez arrives in Ethiopia at the start of a six-year mission.

👑 **1524** The Ottomans put down an attempt by Egypt's governor Ahmad Pasha al-Khair to set himself up as an independent ruler.

👑 **1526** The ruler of the West African Kingdom of Kongo tries unsuccesfully to expel the Portuguese.

WESTERN ASIA

👑 **1520** Suleiman I, "the Magnificent," succeeds his father Selim as Ottoman sultan.

✕ **1521** Suleiman launches a major invasion of the Kingdom of Hungary.

👑 **1523** Ibrahim Pasha, born Greek and sold into slavery by pirates, becomes Suleiman's grand vizier.

SOUTH & CENTRAL ASIA

✕ **1524** The Mughal leader Babur seizes Lahore.

✕ **1526** Babur defeats the sultan of Delhi at the Battle of Panipat and occupies Delhi and Agra.

✕ **1525** Babur invades the Punjab.

EAST ASIA & OCEANIA

⊕ **1521** Ferdinand Magellan is killed by natives in the Phillipines. His around-the-world voyage continues under his second in command, Sebastiano del Cano.

⊕ **1521** The Portuguese establish a trading post at Amboina in the Moluccas, the famed Spice Islands of Indonesia.

Chinese Ming vase from the reign of the Emperor Shizung.

14

⚔ **1522** Spanish forces conquer Guatemala.

⊕ **1522** Pascual de Andagoya leads a land expedition from Panama to Peru.

⊕ **1522** Francisco Montano ascends Mt. Popocatapetl in Mexico.

☀ **1529** The Franciscan friar Bernardino de Sahagún starts his mission in Mexico.

AMERICAS

⊕ **1522** Magellan's flagship the *Victoria*, now under the command of Sebastiano del Cano, returns to Spain, completing the first circumnavigation of the world.

👑 **1523** Gustavus Vasa, leader of Swedish resistance to Danish rule, comes to power as Gustavus I.

⚔ **1525** French forces in Italy are routed at the Battle of Pavia. King Francis I is taken prisoner.

☀ **1525** In Germany the Catholic League is founded to combat Lutheranism.

👑 **1525** Sigismund I of Poland ends the rule of the Teutonic Knights in Prussia.

👑 **1526** The Peasants' War in Germany ends in brutal suppression.

⚔ **1526** Ottoman forces defeat the Hungarian army at the Battle of Mohacs.

☀ **1527** Sweden opts for Lutheranism, cutting its ties to the papacy.

⚔ **1527** Mutinous imperial forces sack Rome, imprisoning Pope Clement VII and killing 4,000 inhabitants.

☀ **1528** Finland adopts the Lutheran faith.

⚔ **1529** Ottoman forces under Suleiman the Magnificent fail to take Vienna after a 17-day siege.

EUROPE

⚔ **1529** The buccaneer Khayr ad-Din, known in the West as Barbarossa, seizes Algiers with Ottoman aid.

Barbarossa rose to fame attacking Christian shipping in the Mediterranean. Capturing Algiers from Spain, he ceded it to the Ottoman sultan, who responded by making him admiral of his fleet.

AFRICA

👑 **1524** Shah Esmail, founder of Persia's Safavid Dynasty, dies. He is succeeded by his 10-year-old son.

WESTERN ASIA

⚔ **1527** Babur defeats the Hindu Rajputs at Khanua, successfully defending his conquests of the previous year.

⚔ **1529** Babur completes the conquest of the Delhi Sultanate as far east as the frontier with Bengal.

SOUTH & CENTRAL ASIA

👑 **1521** Takakuni Masamoto drives the Japanese Shogun Yoshitane out of his capital, Kyoto, further reducing the prestige of the Ashikaga Shogunate.

👑 **1521** A Portuguese envoy, Thomé Pires, arrives at the Chinese court.

👑 **1522** The Portuguese are expelled from China following the piratical activities of Simao d'Andrade and other buccaneers.

👑 **1522** In China the Ming Emperor Shizung begins a long reign (−1567).

⊕ **1526** Portuguese vessels reach New Guinea.

👑 **1529** By the Treaty of Saragossa the Holy Roman Emperor Charles V and the Portuguese divide spheres of interest in East Asia. Portugal retains the Moluccas.

EAST ASIA & OCEANIA

1520–1530 A.D.

15

THE CONQUISTADORS

FOLLOWING THE EUROPEAN DISCOVERY *of the New World, sizable numbers of Spanish soldiers and adventurers crossed the Atlantic Ocean in search of gold and glory. Many went only to their deaths, but other conquistadors—so called from the Spanish word for "conquerors"—helped change the course of history. One group under Hernán Cortés conquered the Aztec Empire of Mexico, while another under Francisco Pizarro made themselves masters of the Inca Empire of Peru. The Hispanic Empire they created in Central and South America lasted for 400 years and made Spain itself for a century or more the wealthiest country in Europe.*

▲ Steel helmets provided protection from enemy slingshots and arrows.

▼ Emissaries of the Aztec emperor greet Hernán Cortés.

Cortés and Pizarro were both younger sons of minor Spanish noblemen who had come to the New World to seek their fortunes. In earlier centuries such men had found employment fighting the Moors who occupied parts of Spain itself, but with the collapse of the last Moorish kingdom in 1492 they were forced to look abroad instead.

Cortés landed in Mexico in 1519 with a force of just 508 soldiers. Crucially, he also had seven small cannons and 16 horses; both were unknown on the American continent at the time. His men had little idea of what they would find on the mainland and were startled to discover a well-organized empire with a capital city, Tenochtitlán, that was bigger than Madrid or London at the time. The Aztecs had built their empire by force, however, and the newcomers were able to find allies among local peoples eager to throw off their yoke. The Spaniards also benefited from the uncertain response of the Aztec ruler Montezuma II, who initially welcomed them, uncertain whether the strangers with unfamiliar weapons might not be emissaries sent by the gods, as foretold in certain Aztec myths.

Pizarro was equally fortunate to arrive in the Inca lands at a time when they had just been riven by civil war. When the victor, Atahualpa, agreed to meet him and his men, Pizarro's troops took him prisoner, slaughtering his vast retinue of unarmed bodyguards. With the emperor in their hands, the tiny force of 180 Spaniards were able to impose their will on the leaderless millions who had been his subjects.

👑 **1428** The Aztec people become the dominant power in the Valley of Mexico. By the end of the century most of Mexico also accepts their overlordship.

⚔ **1438** Under a new ruler, Pachacutec, the Inca people of Peru embark on a course of military expansion, eventually building an empire stretching from Ecuador into northern Chile.

⚙ **1492** Christopher Columbus crosses the Atlantic Ocean from Spain to discover the New World on its western shores.

👑 **1494** By the Treaty of Tordesillas Spain and Portugal agree to divide control of the New World along a line of longitude 370 leagues (about 1,150 miles/1,850 km) west of the Cape Verde Islands.

⚙ **1500** Under the terms of the treaty the navigator Pedro Alvares Cabral claims Brazil, which lies east of the line, for Portugal.

👑 **1504** Hernán Cortés arrives on the island of Hispaniola from Spain as a 19-year-old fortune-seeker.

⚔ **1511** A Spanish force under Diego de Velazquez occupies Cuba.

⚔ **1519** Spanish conquistadors led by Hernán Cortés land on the Mexican coast and march on the Aztec capital, Tenochtitlán. The Aztec Emperor Montezuma receives the Spaniards as guests, only for them to take him prisoner.

A Mountain of Silver

More than anything else, the lure of gold and silver drew the conquistadors into Central and South America. They were not disappointed with what they found. Cortés sent beautifully crafted examples of Aztec gold- and silverwork back to Spain that became the wonder of Europe. In Peru Atahualpa's subjects filled a hall of his palace with gold to a depth of almost 7 feet (2 m) in a vain attempt to ransom their emperor from his captors. After the conquest the Spaniards found even greater riches in Mt. Potosí (right), a hill in Bolivia that eventually yielded more than 18,000 tons of silver ore. Annual silver fleets carried the treasure back to Spain, which became the wealthiest country in Europe for more than a century until the mines were finally exhausted.

Many conquistadors died in battle or of disease, but a lucky few made vast fortunes. More significantly, they won a vast and wealthy American empire for Spain; rarely have so few people left such a large mark on history.

For the native peoples, though, the Spaniards' triumphs were an almost complete disaster. Thousands died in the fighting, and millions more succumbed to diseases such as smallpox that entered the country with the Spaniards and to which they had no immunity. It has been estimated that the population of Mexico fell from 25 million to 2.7 million in the years after the conquest, while that of Peru plummeted from 9 million to 1.3 million.

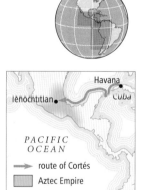

route of Cortés
Aztec Empire

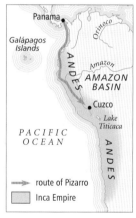

route of Pizarro
Inca Empire

◀ The Aztec Empire that Cortés conquered occupied much of modern Mexico (far left); his troops set out from Cuba. Pizarro's forces sailed south from Panama, landing in northern Peru (near left). Summoned to meet the Inca ruler Atahualpa, Pizarro accepted, only to stage a surprise attack. By taking Atahualpa prisoner, he made himself master of the Inca Empire and its captial, Cuzco.

⚔ **1520** The citizens of Tenochtitlán revolt, killing Montezuma and temporarily driving out the Spanish.

⚔ **1521** Cortés returns with reinforcements to take Tenochtitlán after an eight-week siege, winning control of the Aztec Empire for Spain.

⚔ **1525** In the Inca lands civil war breaks out between rival contenders for the throne.

⊕ **1530** Portuguese colonists found the first permanent settlements in Brazil.

⚔ **1532** Atahualpa emerges victorious from the Inca civil war only to be taken captive by Spanish conquistadors under Francisco Pizarro, who have staged a landing on the Peruvian coast.

⚔ **1533** Atahualpa is executed on Pizarro's orders. The conquistadors take control of the Inca capital Cuzco.

👑 **1535** Pizarro founds a new capital, Lima, on the Peruvian coast.

👑 **1535** The Holy Roman Emperor Charles V sends a viceroy to rule Mexico, now called New Spain, in his name.

👑 **1541** Pizarro is assassinated by rival conquistadors.

👑 **1542** A Spanish viceroy arrives in Lima to take control of Peru, bringing the era of the conquistadors to an end.

1530–1540 A.D.

AMERICAS

⚙ **1530** The Portuguese found towns at São Vicente and São Paulo, their first colonies in Brazil.

⚔ **1532** The Spanish conquistador Francisco Pizarro conquers Peru and captures the last Inca ruler, Atahualpa, who is executed a year later.

⚙ **1534** The Portuguese ship the first African slaves to Brazil.

⚙ **1534** French explorer Jacques Cartier is the first European to enter the St. Lawrence River; returning a year later, he reaches the future sites of Montreal and Quebec (–1535).

EUROPE

👑 **1530** Ten years after assuming the title, Charles V is crowned Holy Roman emperor at Bologna, Italy; he will be the last one to have a papal coronation.

⚔ **1531** A Catholic Swiss army defeats the Protestants of Zurich at the Battle of Kappel. The Swiss reformer Ulrich Zwingli is one of the dead.

☀ **1531** German Protestant princes form the Schmalkaldic League to resist the attempts of Charles V to reintroduce Catholicism.

📖 **1532** François Rabelais, French monk and physician, publishes his two great satirical masterpieces, *Pantagruel* and *Gargantua* (–1534).

👑 **1533** King Henry VIII of England divorces his first wife Catherine of Aragon, leaving him free to marry Anne Boleyn. As a result, he is excommunicated by the pope.

AFRICA

⚔ **1531** Muslim leader Ahmad Gran goes to war against the Christian rulers of Ethiopia, winning much land.

An Italian medal depicts the flagship of the Genoese admiral Andrea Doria.

WESTERN ASIA

⚔ **1534** Suleiman I invades the Safavid Empire and takes Baghdad, which becomes part of the Ottoman Empire.

👑 **1536** Suleiman I forms an alliance with King Francis I of France against the Hapsburg Empire.

⚔ **1538** The Ottoman navy defeats a Christian fleet at Prevesa, off the west coast of Greece.

SOUTH & CENTRAL ASIA

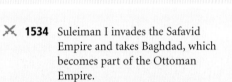

The Mughal Emperor Humayun, shown in this painting on a hunting expedition, inherited the Mughal Empire from his father Babur, lost it to the Afghans, then 15 years later won it back. He spent the intervening years first in the wilderness of Sind then in Persia, whose Shah Tahmasp provided him with the forces to regain his kingdom. He had little time to enjoy his restoration, dying six months later.

👑 **c.1530** The Nakaya Dynasty frees itself from the Vijayanagar Empire of southern India and becomes a great patron of Hindu temple construction.

👑 **1530** Humayun becomes Mughal emperor of India on the death of his father Babur, but has to share his lands with his brothers.

EAST ASIA & OCEANIA

👑 **c.1530** Shizung, Ming emperor of China, largely withdraws from government to concentrate on alchemy.

👑 **1533** The Dai Viet Kingdom of Indochina fragments into a number of small states.

⊕ **1535** Pizarro founds the city of Lima as the Spanish capital in Peru.

☀ **1538** The Spanish establish an archbishopric at Bogota, Colombia, the first in South America.

⊕ **1539** Conquistador Hernando de Soto embarks on a journey of exploration that will take him through Florida and Georgia in search of gold.

Cartier explores the St. Lawrence River, as shown in a 19th-century painting.

☀ **1535** The Anabaptists, a strict Protestant sect, seize control of Münster, Germany, and prophesy the end of the world.

🌑 **1537** Cosimo I de Medici, a great patron of the arts, becomes duke of Florence.

☀ **1535** Henry VIII assumes the title of supreme governor of the Church of England.

☀ **1536** William Tyndale, translator of the Bible into English, is burned at the stake for heresy.

📖 **1539** Agnolo Bronzino, a leading exponent of the Mannerist style, becomes court painter to Cosimo de Medici.

✗ **1534** Khayr ad-Din Barbarossa captures the North African stronghold of Tunis for the Ottomans.

✗ **1535** Andrea Doria, a Genoese admiral in the service of Charles V, drives the Ottomans out of Tunis.

✗ **1535** By this time Ahmad Gran controls most of Ethiopia; Christian resistance continues in the mountain areas.

✗ **1538** An Ottoman naval expedition to the Indian Ocean conquers Aden and brings the whole of the Red Sea coast of Arabia under Ottoman rule.

☀ **1539** Sinan, the most famous of all Islamic architects, becomes chief of the Corps of Royal Architects under Suleiman I.

Sinan's masterpiece, the Suleimaniye Mosque in Istanbul.

🌑 **1535** The Portuguese fortify Diu on the coast of India.

✗ **1538** An Ottoman navy on service in the Indian Ocean combines with a Gujarati army to attack Diu and expel the Portuguese.

✗ **1539** Sher Shah Sur, an Afghan chieftain, rebels against Humayun and conquers Bengal.

📖 **1539** Guru Nanak, the founder of the Sikh religion, dies.

🌑 **1539** Tabinshweti of the Toungou Dynasty captures Pegu, capital of the Mon Dynasty, and begins to unify Burma (modern Myanmar).

AMERICAS

EUROPE

AFRICA

WESTERN ASIA

SOUTH & CENTRAL ASIA

EAST ASIA & OCEANIA

1530–1540 A.D.

THE RENAISSANCE

▲ Probably the world's most famous painting, the *Mona Lisa* owes its alternative name, the *Gioconda*, to its subject, the wife of the Marquis del Giocondo. Painted by Leonardo da Vinci, the work is a masterpiece of Italian Renaissance art.

THE WORD "RENAISSANCE" MEANS REBIRTH. *It refers to an artistic and cultural movement that arose in northern Italy in the 14th century and had spread throughout Europe by the mid-16th century. Historians today recognize in the Renaissance a period of transformation that brought an end to the medieval era, opening the way to new achievements in learning and science that led eventually to the 18th-century Enlightenment. In its origins, however, the Renaissance was backward-looking, seeking inspiration in the art and literature of the classical worlds of Greece and Rome.*

There had been revivals of interest in the classical past before—at the court of the Emperor Charlemagne in the 8th century, for example, and in the 12th century with the rediscovery of the works of Aristotle. One new factor in the 14th and 15th centuries was the decline and collapse of the Byzantine Empire. Well before the fall of Constantinople to the Turks in 1453, Greek scholars had taken large numbers of classical Greek manuscripts for safety to Italy. Previously unknown in the West, these works led to the development of new branches of study, such as mathematics, geography, medicine, and philosophy.

By the early 15th century Italian cities such as Florence, Ferrara, Urbino, Venice, and Milan had become wealthy through international trade and banking. They were hotspots of creativity, where artists and craftsmen such as the architects Alberti

and Brunelleschi and the painters Donatello and Masaccio were developing new styles of painting, decoration, and architecture based on the ideals of the past. As interest in the classical world revived, members of the powerful families that ruled these cities, such as the Medici of Florence and the Sforza of Milan, became great patrons of the arts. They built libraries and churches in the classical style, with an ordered use of columns and symmetry. They also endowed universities that stimulated scholarship, and commissioned portraits and medals of themselves that often showed them as Roman emperors. Partly through the new medium of printing and partly as a result of the wars that brought rulers such as the Emperor Charles V and Francis I of France to Italy, the influence of the Renaissance traveled rapidly outside Italy to all the courts of Europe.

📖 **c.1420** The architect Brunelleschi, the sculptor Donatello, and the painter Masaccio—all important figures in the art of the early Renaissance—are at work in Florence.

📖 **1434** Cosimo de Medici begins a 30-year domination of Florence.

📖 **1440** The Platonic Academy is founded in Florence.

👑 **1450** Francesco Sforza becomes ruler of Milan.

📖 **1485** Sandro Botticelli paints *The Birth of Venus*.

📖 **1505** Albrecht Dürer, German artist and engraver, is present in Venice (–1506).

📖 **1506** Leonardo da Vinci completes his most famous painting, the *Mona Lisa*.

📖 **1508** Michelangelo paints the ceiling of the Sistine Chapel (–1512).

📖 **1508** The painter Raphael moves to Rome and is employed by Pope Julian II to decorate the papal chambers in the Vatican (–1509).

📖 **1509** Erasmus publishes *In Praise of Folly*.

📖 **1513** Niccolo Machiavelli publishes *The Prince*, a handbook for Renaissance monarchs.

📖 **1516** Sir Thomas More writes *Utopia*, in which he describes an imaginary land with an ideal form of government.

📖 **1519** Leonardo da Vinci dies in France while working for Francis I.

📖 **1519** Construction begins on the Château of Chambord, the first building in France in the new Renaissance style.

📖 **1532** Francis I invites Italian painters to his palace at Fontainebleau.

✳ **1543** Nicolaus Copernicus's *On the Revolutions of the Heavenly Bodies* is published, setting the sun at the center of the universe.

📖 **1547** Michelangelo is appointed architect of St. Peter's in Rome.

📖 **c.1550** Giorgio Vasari publishes the *Lives of the Artists*—biographies of the great Renaissance painters.

The scholars of the New Learning, as it was called, challenged the rigid authority of the medieval church. They found inspiration in the works of Plato and other classical writers, and were known as humanists, reflecting their people-centered view of the universe. In art the influence of humanist ideas called for a return to a more realistic depiction of nature, as seen in the works of Leonardo da Vinci (1452–1519). As well as a painter and sculptor, he was an architect and engineer, and his notebooks reveal an immensely inventive mind, way ahead of his time in investigating biology, anatomy, mechanics, and aerodynamics.

▲ In the 16th century Renaissance styles of art and architecture moved north of the Alps, as shown by the Château of Chambord, built for France's King Francis I from 1519 on.

▼ Made rich by trade, Renaissance Italy was a fragmented land of rival city-states that competed with one another for the services of the finest artists and architects.

Erasmus of Rotterdam

If Leonardo da Vinci was the outstanding all-round genius of the Renaissance, Desiderius Erasmus (1466–1536) was its most famous scholar. Born in Rotterdam in the Netherlands, Erasmus became a monk and later went to study in Paris. There he turned against the rigid scholasticism of his youth, embracing instead the new doctrine of humanism, which stressed the power of human reason. He traveled widely, spending time at England's Oxford and Cambridge among other universities, and corresponded with Europe's foremost scholars. He was one of the first popular writers of the age of printing—his most famous work, *In Praise of Folly*, went into 43 editions in his lifetime. He also published a best-selling book of *Adagia* (literally "adages") as well as scholarly editions of classical texts. Erasmus was strongly critical of the abuses of the Catholic church, but he took no part in the Reformation and later attacked Luther for his extreme views.

major cultural center

Italy in the mid 16th century

- Genoese territory
- Papal States
- Spanish Hapsburg lands
- Venetian territory
- other Italian states

VENICE
Asolo
Trieste
Vicenza
MILAN
Verona
Venice
Milan
Turin
SAVOY
Pavia
Mantua
Padua
Cremona
Sabbioneta
Parma
Ferrara
Pola
Carpi
Genoa
Bologna
Zara
GENOA
Pisa
Florence
Urbino
Nice
FLORENCE
PAPAL
Siena
STATES
Ligurian
Piombino
SIENA
Perugia
Sea
Ragusa
Viterbo
Adriatic
Corsica
Sea
Ajaccio
Rome
KINGDOM OF
NAPLES
Benevento
Naples
Salerno
Lecce
KINGDOM OF
SARDINIA
Tyrrhenian Sea
Cagliari
Palermo
Reggio
KINGDOM OF
SICILY
Catania
Ionian Sea
Tunis
Pantelleria

0   200 km
0   150 mi

AMERICAS

⊛ **1540** Pedro de Valdivia establishes a Spanish colony at Santiago de Chile.

⊛ **1540** Francisco Vázquez de Coronado leads an expedition into what is now the American Southwest

⊛ **1541** Hernando de Soto and his party, pushing westward across Georgia, discover the Mississippi River.

⊛ **1541** Francisco Pizarro is hacked to death by rival conquistadors in Peru.

⊛ **1541** Marooned in the Upper Amazon after exploring eastward over the Andes Mountains, Francisco de Orellanas and his men float on rafts downriver to the Atlantic.

👑 **1542** By the Laws of the Indies the Spanish crown abolishes *encomienda*—the right of colonists to exact tribute and labor from Native Americans.

👑 **1542** An *audiencia*—a Spanish court with governing powers—is established in Lima, Peru

EUROPE

☀ **1540** The Society of Jesus (the Jesuit order) is given official recognition by Pope Paul III.

☀ **1541** John Calvin begins preaching as chief pastor in Geneva, Switzerland.

✕ **1542** War breaks out between England and France (–1546).

✕ **1543** Hungary is conquered by the Ottoman Turks.

As shown here in a contemporary illustration, the Polish astronomer Nicolaus Copernicus pioneered the view that the planets moved around the sun; earlier authorities had followed the classical writer Ptolemy of Alexandria in viewing the Earth as the center of the universe. A lifelong churchman, Copernicus only agreed to publish his controversial views shortly before his death in 1543.

AFRICA

✕ **1540** Under the command of Barbarossa the Ottoman navy defeats Charles V's fleet off Crete.

✕ **1541** Barbarossa inflicts a second defeat on the Christians off Algiers.

✕ **1542** With Portuguese aid, Ethiopia's King Lebna Denegel takes the offensive against Ahmad Gran.

WESTERN ASIA

👑 **1540** The death of Ubayd Allah Kahn puts an end to Uzbek raids on the eastern provinces of Safavid Persia.

👑 **1547** The Ottoman Sultan Suleiman the Magnificent and Ferdinand of Austria sign a peace treaty.

👑 **1547** The Ottomans take control of the port of Basra in what is now Iraq. Former pirate Piri Reis takes command of the Ottoman Indian Ocean fleet.

SOUTH & CENTRAL ASIA

✕ **1540** The Afghan Sher Shah Sur defeats the Mughal Emperor Humayun and seizes power in Delhi.

☀ **1542** St. Francis Xavier begins his mission to Goa in western India.

✕ **1543** Sher Shah Sur extends his realm to the Indian Ocean.

✕ **1543** In Sri Lanka Portuguese colonists join the native Kingdom of Kotte in a disastrous attempted invasion of the northern Kingdom of Kandy.

EAST ASIA & OCEANIA

✕ **1541** King Tabinshweti of Toungou completes his conquest of the Mon Dynasty to make himself ruler of a reunited Burma (Myanmar).

👑 **1542** Sunan Gunung Jati founds Banten on the Sunda Strait. The new Islamic state will soon come to dominate the neighboring Hindu kingdoms of western Java.

⊛ **1542** A group of Portuguese sailors making an accidental landfall become the first Europeans to set foot on Japanese soil.

Bartolomé de las Casas campaigned for the humane treatment of indigenous peoples.

⊕ **1545** A typhus epidemic in New Spain claims an estimated 100,000 native lives, along with those of a few European settlers.

⊕ **1545** The richest silver mine in the Americas opens at Potosí in what is now Bolivia.

⊕ **1545** Bartolomé de las Casas founds a utopian community based on partnership between Europeans and Indians at Verapaz in Honduras.

👑 **1549** Tomé de Sousa is sent from Portugal to govern Brazil.

AMERICAS

⊕ **1543** Nicolaus Copernicus publishes *De Revolutionibus Orbium Coelestium* ("On the Revolutions of the Heavenly Bodies"), suggesting that the planets orbit the sun.

⊕ **1543** Andreas Vesalius's *De Humani Corporis Fabrica* ("On the Structure of the Human Body"), widely regarded as the founding work of modern anatomical science, is published.

☀ **1545** The Council of Trent begins in Italy, launching the Counter-Reformation.

✕ **1546** The Anglo-French War ends with England taking the French port of Boulogne.

👑 **1547** Ivan IV, "the Terrible," becomes the first czar of Russia.

👑 **1547** Francis I of France dies, to be succeeded by his son, Henry II.

✕ **1547** Charles V's general in the Netherlands, the duke of Alba, gains a decisive victory over the Schmalkaldic League at the Battle of Mühlberg.

✕ **1549** War breaks out again between England and France.

EUROPE

✕ **1543** Ahmad Gran is killed in battle, bringing to an end the Muslim attempt to take over Ethiopia.

👑 **1543** Afonso I of Kongo dies, leaving his kingdom open to the slave trade's destabilizing influence.

AFRICA

✕ **1548** Despite the help of a huge Ottoman army, Alqas Mirza, governor of Khurasan, fails to overthrow his brother, Persia's Shah Tahmasp.

✕ **1548** The Ottoman admiral Piri Reis takes Aden back from the Portuguese.

Persia's Shah Tahmasp receives an ambassador in his palace.

👑 **1545** Sher Shah Sur takes Chitor, stronghold of the Rajputs, effectively completing his conquest of Rajasthan. He dies soon after, to be succeeded by his son Islam Shah.

✕ **1546** The Ottoman Turks besiege the Gujarati port of Diu.

WESTERN ASIA

SOUTH & CENTRAL ASIA

✕ **1545** King Prajai of Ayutthaya (Thailand) invades Chiengmai in northwestern Thailand. He is eventually sent packing by the Laotian army.

✕ **1548** Portuguese mercenaries repulse an attack by Tabinshweti of Burma on Ayutthaya. The ruler is assassinated soon after.

☀ **1549** Jesuit missionaries led by St. Francis Xavier reach Japan.

EAST ASIA & OCEANIA

1540–1550 A.D.

THE REFORMATION

PROTESTANTISM WAS BORN OF *Martin Luther's attempt to reform the Catholic church, which in his eyes was riddled with greed and corruption. The religious upheavals that followed his call split the unity of Western Christendom and unleashed a century and a half of bitter warfare and vicious persecution. At a time when religion was an essential part of everyday life, the turmoil in the church affected all of Europe.*

▲ In 1520 Pope Leo X issued a papal bull (decree), shown above, condemning the views of Martin Luther as heretical. When Luther responded by burning the document, he was excommunicated (barred) from the Catholic church. The Reformation was under way.

▶ As the map shows, Protestantism in its Lutheran, Calvinist, and Anglican forms was at first mostly confined to northern Europe; the south remained loyal to the pope.

majority faith 1550
- Anglican
- Catholic
- Calvinist
- Lutheran
- Muslim
- Orthodox
- mixed

※ **1517** Martin Luther posts his 95 Theses criticizing church abuses on the door of Wittenberg Cathedral in Germany.

※ **1525** William Tyndale produces an English translation of the Greek New Testament.

※ **1529** Henry VIII begins a dispute with Pope Clement VII over his wish to divorce Catherine of Aragon.

※ **1533** Henry VIII marries Anne Boleyn in defiance of Pope Clement VII. He is promptly excommunicated (expelled from the Catholic church).

※ **1534** Henry VIII breaks with Rome, establishing the Church of England.

※ **1534** Luther completes his German translation of the Bible. Ignatius of Loyola founds the Society of Jesus (the Jesuits).

※ **1536** John Calvin publishes the *Institutes of the Christian Religion*.

※ **1540** The Society of Jesus receives official recognition from Pope Paul III. It will become a spearhead of the Counter-Reformation.

※ **1541** Calvin is appointed chief pastor in Geneva.

※ **1542** The Jesuit missionary St. Francis Xavier reaches Goa, western India.

※ **1545** Catholic prelates meet to discuss church reform at the Council of Trent in northern Italy (−1563).

※ **1549** St. Francis Xavier's missionaries reach Japan.

※ **1549** The Protestant *Book of Common Prayer* is published for use in all English churches.

♛ **1553** Mary I becomes queen of England, which reverts to the Catholic faith. Many Protestants are tortured and killed in the persecution that follows.

Some historians maintain that the Catholic church has been in a state of rolling reformation since its earliest times: There was no shortage of reformers in the medieval period. But the crisis that began when the German monk Martin Luther nailed his 95 Theses criticizing church abuses to the door of Wittenberg Cathedral in 1517 represented a change of attitude on an altogether different scale. Outraged at the sale of indulgences—documents sold for cash to purchase the forgiveness of sins—Luther had boiled over in his anger at a church that seemed more concerned with earthly wealth and power than heavenly salvation.

Luther is generally considered to have been the first "Protestant," the catchall name given to all the various groups and individuals who followed his lead and eventually broke with the Catholic church. His belief that the structures of the church only interfered between individual men and women and their God quickly struck a chord throughout Germany and much of northern Europe. The spirit of revolt spread like wildfire, and the attack that Luther had launched on the pope's authority quickly broadened into a split.

Many of the protestors who took up the cause of reform were sincere believers like Luther himself, shocked by clerical misconduct. Others were more opportunistic. Henry VIII of England first denounced Luther's views, then underwent a change of heart when the pope refused to grant him a divorce from his marriage. The Church of England that he established was at first Catholic in everything but obedience to Rome, which Henry renounced.

Luther's own objections were to the institutions of the church and the conduct of its clergy; his faith in its central tenets remained unchanged. In Geneva, however, the French preacher John Calvin rethought Christian theology altogether, promoting a theological system that was severe and strongly Bible based. In his view the faithful, or "elect," would be saved, but sinners would be cast into hell forever: He even argued that God knew in advance which group was which, and that some people were thus predestined to be damned. In English-speaking countries his followers became known as Puritans, famed for their strict personal morality and their often intolerant attitude to those who did not share their beliefs.

The political effect of the Reformation was to split first Europe and later other parts of the world into opposing Protestant and Catholic camps. Protestants were persecuted in Catholic lands, Catholics in the growing number of Protestant ones, but many braved torture and death rather than surrender their beliefs.

Meanwhile, thoughtful Catholics quickly came to realize that there was some justice in Luther's complaints. Firm in their loyalty to the pope, they sought to combat the Protestants by cleansing the church of abuses from within. Leading churchmen met at the Council of Trent (1545–1563) to draft the necessary reforms, and a group of dedicated Catholic writers, artists, and priests mobilized to reinvigorate the faith in the intellectual and spiritual movement called the Counter-Reformation.

▲ The French reformer John Calvin preached a strict version of Protestantism that became a model for the Puritans. He got the opportunity to put his ideas into practice in Geneva in Switzerland, serving as its chief pastor for 28 years.

The Good Book

Today Christians take it for granted that reading the Bible is a pious duty: Prior to the Reformation it was regarded as an activity best left to priests. The Catholic church argued that there was less likelihood of error if the general public had the word of God interpreted for them by its own trained ministers. Biblical study was anyway difficult for nonscholars, for the only generally available copies of the sacred texts were in Latin, Greek, or Hebrew, languages that few ordinary citizens could understand. Reformers like Martin Luther felt that the Church's policy was obstructing the spreading of the Christian message. They sought to encourage access to the Bible by producing texts in the "vernacular"—the commonly spoken languages of their countries. Luther's own German translation (right) appeared in 1534. The church authorities fiercely resisted such efforts. William Tyndale, the English translator, was first forced into exile and eventually burned at the stake.

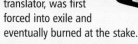

AMERICAS

📖 **1551** The first universities in the Americas are established in Mexico City and in Lima, Peru.

☀ **1551** Brazil gets its first bishop, based in Bahia and answerable to the archbishop of Lisbon.

📖 **1552** Bartolomé de las Casas's indictment of New World colonialism, *A Brief Account of the Destruction of the Indies*, is published in book form.

EUROPE

⚔ **1550** The Anglo–French War ends with France taking Boulogne back from the English.

⚔ **1552** The Russians conquer the former Mongol Khanate of Khazan, opening the way for later ventures across the Urals into Siberia.

☀ **1553** Mary I restores Catholicism as the state religion of England. Many Protestants are martyred for their faith, earning the queen the nickname "Bloody Mary."

The wealth flooding into Spain from its American colonies launched a golden age and made the Spanish ruler, Philip II, the most powerful king in Europe. Coming to power in 1556, Philip also inherited the Spanish Netherlands and lands in Italy; in 1580 he acceded to the Portuguese throne. A champion of Catholicism, Philip took on Protestant rebels in the Netherlands as well as England's Queen Elizabeth I, sending the Spanish Armada against her in 1588; ultimately, neither campaign was successful. In Spain Philip put down a revolt of the Moriscos (Christianized Muslims) between 1568 and 1570, but his incessant wars and the taxes needed to pay for them left the country bankrupt on his death in 1598.

AFRICA

⚔ **1550** The Marrakech warlord al-Shaykh takes Fez to make his Saadi Dynasty masters of Morocco.

⚔ **1551** The Ottoman Turks take Tripoli from the Knights Hospitallers.

👑 **1555** Diogo I, Christian king of Kongo, quarrels with his Portuguese backers, expelling all Portuguese nationals from his kingdom.

WESTERN ASIA

👑 **1551** Ottoman admiral Piri Reis expels the Portuguese from Muscat.

⚔ **1553** Suleiman I mounts a second invasion of Persia, ended by the Treaty of Amasya (–1555).

👑 **1553** Suspecting conspiracy, Suleiman orders the execution of his son Mustafa.

⚔ **1555** A rebellion by supporters of Mustafa is put down in Anatolia.

👑 **1556** Shah Tahmasp's son Esmail is appointed governor of Khorasan but promptly falls under suspicion of plotting a coup. The future shah will spend the next 19 years of his life in prison.

SOUTH & CENTRAL ASIA

⚔ **1551** Portuguese colonists renew their alliance with the Kingdom of Kotte in southwestern Sri Lanka, this time to attack neighboring Sitavaka.

👑 **1555** India's second Mughal emperor, Humayun, occupies Lahore and goes on to reestablish Mughal power in Delhi.

👑 **1555** Humayun dies and is succeeded by his 13-year-old son Akbar, who rules under the supervision of a regent, Bairam Khan.

EAST ASIA & OCEANIA

👑 **c.1550** Cambodia's King Anga Chan rediscovers the ruined Khmer capital of Angkor Wat in the jungle. His attempt to restore it to its former splendor is doomed to failure.

👑 **1551** In the confusion following the assassination of Tabinshweti, Bayinnaung becomes king of Burma.

☀ **1552** The missionary St. Francis Xavier dies on a small island off Macao after repeated, unsuccessful attempts to reach the Chinese mainland.

⚔ **1554** Bayinnaung invades the Laotian territory of Chiangmai, annexing it after a four-year war (–1558).

Bayinnaung's palace at Bago in Burma (Myanmar).

☀️ **1554** Jesuit priests at odds with the bishop of Bahia leave for the São Vicente region: The settlement they found will eventually grow into the city of São Paulo.

👑 **1559** The *audiencia* of Charcas is established, centered on what is now Bolivia but extending south to include Paraguay, Uruguay, and Argentina.

👑 **1559** A Spanish expedition under Tristán de Luna seeks unsuccessfully to colonize the Carolinas (–1561).

AMERICAS

👑 **1555** The Peace of Augsburg is signed. In his capacity as Holy Roman emperor Charles V acknowledges the right of local German rulers within the empire to decide the official religion in their territories.

👑 **1556** Charles V abdicates. His son Philip II inherits Spain with the Netherlands, Naples, and Milan, while the Hapsburg lands in Central Europe together with the title of Holy Roman emperor go to Charles's brother Ferdinand.

✕ **1559** The Treaty of Cateau-Cambrésis brings an end to almost 70 years of on–off war between France and the Hapsburgs; France abandons all its Italian claims. The treaty also concludes hostilities between France and England, confirming England's loss of Calais, its last foothold in France.

☀️ **1556** In England the archbishop of Canterbury, Thomas Cranmer, is burned at the stake for his Protestant beliefs despite a series of recantations that he retracts in his last moments.

👑 **1558** Mary I dies, and Elizabeth I is crowned queen of England.

☀️ **1559** The first national synod (council) of French Protestants ("Huguenots") is held.

EUROPE

👑 **1557** The Ottoman Turks have al-Shaykh assassinated but cannot check Morocco's revival under his Saadi successors.

👑 **1559** The Portuguese initiate contacts with Ndambi, king of Ndongo in what is now Angola.

AFRICA

☀️ **1556** Istanbul's Suleimaniye Mosque is inaugurated after being under construction for six years.

✕ **1557** The Ottoman navy recaptures the Red Sea ports previously taken by Portugal.

👑 **1559** Though their father is still alive, Suleiman's sons Bayezid and Selim take up arms to contest the succession. Bayezid flees to Iran, seeking protection from Shah Tahmasp

WESTERN ASIA

✕ **1556** Akbar's authority as emperor is confirmed by a Mughal victory over a Hindu army at Panipat in northern India.

SOUTH & CENTRAL ASIA

✵ **1557** A Portuguese trading settlement is established on the coast of mainland China at Macao.

👑 **1558** Lan Na in Ayutthaya (modern Thailand) becomes a subject state of Bayinnaung's Burmese Empire.

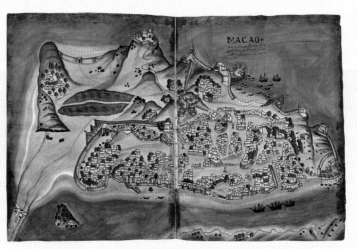

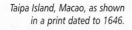

Taipa Island, Macao, as shown in a print dated to 1646.

EAST ASIA & OCEANIA

SULEIMAN THE MAGNIFICENT

I N THE TURKISH OTTOMAN EMPIRE *his own subjects called him "Suleiman the Lawgiver" in honor of his efforts to protect the individual from the excesses of arbitrary rule. To the West, though, he has always been "Suleiman the Magnificent." The title was awarded grudgingly—he was a bitter foe of Christendom—but his greatness could not be ignored. The tragedy for the Ottoman Empire was that his reign represented a culmination: Thereafter there would be only a long decline.*

▲ A gold coin from the time of Suleiman the Magnificent describes the Ottoman sultan as "Lord of might and victory by land and sea." Under his rule Ottoman power stretched from the Arabian Sea almost to the Straits of Gibraltar.

▶ An Ottoman gouache (watercolor) painting shows Suleiman's forces arrayed outside Belgrade in 1521. The city fell to his troops after weeks of bombardment and 20 massed attacks.

The future Suleiman I was still a teenager when his father became sultan. Selim was to prove a highly effective ruler, defeating the Ottomans' chief eastern rival, the Safavid ruler of Persia, at Chaldiran in 1514 and conquering the Mamelukes to win Egypt and Syria two years later. Yet his means of winning and holding onto power justified the name that history was to give him: "Selim the Grim." He probably had his own father poisoned in his eagerness to inherit the throne; he certainly had his two elder brothers garroted and their five sons strangled to remove rival claimants. He also ordered the massacre of 40,000 Muslim heretics in eastern Anatolia to underline his role as the protector of Islamic orthodoxy.

When Suleiman came to the throne in 1520, he therefore inherited a tradition of despotic absolutism as well as a mighty empire. He was the tenth ruler of the Ottoman Dynasty, which had first risen to power in northern Anatolia (modern Asiatic Turkey) in the late 13th century. His predecessors had put paid to the Christian Byzantine Empire and forged a realm that incorporated Turkey and the Balkan lands as well as the eastern Mediterranean seaboard and Egypt.

Suleiman's first act on becoming sultan was to introduce sweeping reforms to the legal system,

<hr>

👑 **c.1494** Birth of Suleiman.

👑 **1511** Suleiman's father becomes Sultan Selim I.

👑 **1520** Suleiman becomes Ottoman sultan after his father's death from cancer.

⚔ **1521** Suleiman captures Belgrade from the Hungarians.

⚔ **1522** The island of Rhodes is taken.

⚔ **1534** The Ottoman navy is placed under the command of Barbarossa.

👑 **1536** The Grand Vizier Ibrahim is summarily executed.

⚔ **1543** In alliance with France the Ottoman fleet sacks Nice, held at the time by an ally of the Holy Roman emperor.

⚔ **1544** Barbarossa's fleet raids towns along the Italian coast.

👑 **1547** Suleiman agrees to a five-year truce with Emperor Ferdinand of Austria, allowing him to campaign in the east against Persia.

👑 **1553** Suleiman orders the murder of his son, Mustafa, suspected of conspiring against him.

⚔ **1559** Suleiman's sons Selim and Bayezid begin fighting over the succession.

👑 **1561** Bayezid is executed on his father's orders.

⚔ **1565** The island of Malta successfully resists an Ottoman siege.

👑 **1566** Death of Suleiman. He is succeeded by his son, Selim II.

The Suleimaniye Mosque

"Whoever builds a mosque, desiring thereby God's pleasure, God builds the like for him in paradise." The Prophet Muhammad's words no doubt ran through the minds of the builders of Istanbul's Suleimaniye Mosque. Designed by Suleiman's chief architect Sinan and built between 1548 and 1557, it was intended not just to reflect God's glory but also to proclaim the wealth and power of the Ottoman Dynasty and to confirm the sultan's status as "God's shadow on earth." The Suleimaniye was always more than simply a place of worship: It was also a house of Islamic culture, with colleges and libraries attached, and a place of charity, with its own hospital and school and a soup kitchen to feed the poor. Distributions of food from the mosques played a vital political role, helping ease the empire through times of economic hardship.

introducing new laws to protect his subjects from arbitrarily imposed taxes, trade restrictions, and land confiscations. He extended the protection of the law not just to Muslims but also to other religious groups. Western visitors were staggered by the tolerance they found in Ottoman society under Suleiman. "He constrains no one," enthused a French traveler, "but permits everyone to live as his conscience dictates."

Abroad, Suleiman's policy was aggressive. In 1521 he captured Belgrade; the next year he seized the strategic island of Rhodes in the Aegean. In 1529 he terrified Europe by besieging Vienna; although that attempt was unsuccessful, he completed the conquest of Hungary in 1543. Earlier Ottoman sultans had been hampered by a lack of sea power, a weakness Suleiman addressed. Under the command of Khayr ad-Din Barbarossa ("Redbeard"), a North African corsair, his fleet harried Western shipping in the Mediterranean. Allying with France's Francis I against the Emperor Charles V, Barbarossa's fleet destroyed Nice, and Turkish Muslims wintered in Toulon.

At home Suleiman could be ruthless as well as just. In 1536 he had his Grand Vizier Ibrahim, long his most trusted adviser, executed—Suleiman's beloved Russian wife Roxelana is said to have had resented the vizier's power. In 1553 he ordered the murder of his own son Mustafa, whom he thought was conspiring against his rule.

Suleiman was to be last of the great Ottomans; his successor on his death in 1566 went down in history as "Selim the Sot" for his drunken ways, and some later rulers proved similarly deficient. Even so, the empire Suleiman had helped build was to survive for another 350 years. For that alone he merited the title history bestowed on him of "the Magnificent."

- ■ Ottoman administrative center
- Ottoman Empire 1520
- gains under Suleiman I 1520–66
- Tunis, temporary Ottoman gain 1534–35

| 0 | 1,200 km |
| 0 | 800 mi |

◀ Suleiman extended the Ottoman Empire in all directions. In the west he conquered Hungary; in the east he won Mesopotamia (modern Iraq) from the Persian Safavids. To the south he extended Ottoman rule from Egypt along the North African coast and down the Red Sea to Aden.

1560–1570 A.D.

AMERICAS

1564 A group of French Calvinists led by Jean Ribault establishes a settlement (Fort Caroline) at the mouth of the St. John's River in northern Florida.

1565 A Spanish expeditionary force wipes out the French outpost at Fort Caroline, Florida, and establishes a new colony along the coast at St. Augustine.

1565 The Portuguese drive the French from their settlement on the Brazilian coast and establish a new one of their own that is the origin of Rio de Janeiro (–1567).

EUROPE

Perhaps the most powerful woman in French history, Catherine de Medici became Queen of France in 1547 as the wife of Henry II. On his death in 1559 she served as regent first for their son Francis II and then, when he in turn died the next year, for the 10-year-old Charles IX. As the nation's true ruler, she became embroiled in the religious wars setting Catholics against the Protestant Huguenots and was considered responsible for the massacre of Huguenot leaders in Paris on St. Bartholmew's Day 1572. Her power waned when a third son, Henry III, came to the throne as an adult in 1574.

1562 The first Huguenot revolt breaks out in western France.

1562 St. Teresa of Avila receives the church's blessing to found the Convent of St. Joseph and a new order of rigorously disciplined Discalced Carmelite nuns.

1563 Work begins on the construction of the Escorial, Philip II's great palace–mausoleum in the mountains outside Madrid.

1561 Sweden conquers Estonia, embarking on what will be a steady campaign of expansionism over the coming decades.

1561 Charles IX inherits the French throne at the age of 13. Real power rests in the hands of his mother, Catherine de Medici.

1565 Malta successfully resists a four-month siege by the Ottoman Turks.

AFRICA

1562 Captain John Hawkins gets the English slave trade under way with a raid up West Africa's Sierra Leone River.

1567 Alvare succeeds Diogo I as king of Kongo, inheriting a kingdom badly weakened by the depredations of the slave trade.

1568 Kongo is devastated by nomadic Jaga raiders, themselves dislodged from home territories farther east by the activities of slavers.

WESTERN ASIA

1561 Shah Tahmasp of Persia surrenders Suleiman's rebellious son Bayezid to the Ottoman ruler in return for a substantial ransom and in order to prevent the possibility of a further war.

1566 Death of Suleiman I, "the Magnificent." He is succeeded by his son Selim II, who will become known as "Selim the Sot." The Ottoman decline is generally held to have started with his accession.

SOUTH & CENTRAL ASIA

1561 Akbar dispenses with the services of his regent and takes the reins as India's third Mughal emperor. Under his rule the empire will enjoy its golden age.

1564 Akbar subdues the Gakkhar rulers of Punjab and the Gonds of eastern India.

The ruins of Chittor Fort, Rajasthan, India.

EAST ASIA & OCEANIA

1560 After a series of floods, droughts, and earthquakes have exacerbated an already deep economic crisis, cuts in army rations spark off a violent mutiny in Nanking, China.

1564 King Bayinnaung of Burma strikes southeast into Ayutthaya (Thailand) and takes the city of that name, which is promptly lost again after a local uprising.

1565 Although claimed for Spain by Magellan in 1521, the Philippines only now receive their first European colonists—and their modern name, in honor of King Philip II.

👑 **1566** Angered by restrictions on their rights over indigenous peoples, colonists in Mexico City conspire to break away from Spanish rule, but their plans are discovered.

☀ **1569** The Spanish introduce the Inquisition to America, setting up tribunals in Mexico City and Lima (–1571).

✕ **1567** Philip II sends the Duke of Alba to Brussells to quell unrest in the Spanish Netherlands, but he succeeds only in sparking an all-out rebellion.

✕ **1569** Moriscos—Muslim Spaniards only nominally converted to Christianity—rise in revolt against Philip II's attempts to force them to abandon their language and culture.

The Escorial was built by Philip II of Spain as a palace–monastery and a burial place for Spanish kings.

👑 **1567** In Scotland the Catholic Mary Queen of Scots is ousted by a confederacy of Protestant lords.

👑 **1569** The Union of Lublin unites Lithuania and Poland under the rule of the Polish King Sigismund II, bringing the enlarged nation into conflict with Russia.

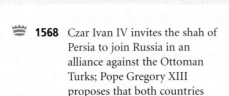

✕ **1569** The Ottoman Turks take Tunis on the North African coast.

✕ **1567** The Zeydis, Shiite heretics in Yemen, take advantage of Selim's weakness to stage an uprising. They are put down but retain a presence in the mountains (–1568).

👑 **1568** Czar Ivan IV invites the shah of Persia to join Russia in an alliance against the Ottoman Turks; Pope Gregory XIII proposes that both countries participate in a "crusade."

✕ **1565** In India the Hindu Vijayanagar Empire is overthrown by the Deccani Sultanates, a Muslim alliance that wins a crushing victory at the Battle of Talikota.

✕ **1568** The Mughal Emperor Akbar destroys the Rajput stronghold of Chittor in Rajasthan after a siege; about 30,000 Rajputs are massacred.

✕ **1569** The last great Rajput fortress, Rathambor, falls to Akbar.

✕ **1565** Relentless raids by Sultan Hairun of Ternate, one of the Molucca Islands (eastern Indonesia), finally drive Christian missionaries out of the islands.

👑 **1568** The *daimyo* (warlord) Oda Nobunaga seizes control of the area around Kyoto in Japan, installing Ashikaga Yoshiaki as a puppet shogun in a first step toward the reunification of the country.

👑 **1569** Bayinnaung takes Ayutthaya for a second time, placing it under the rule of a loyal puppet prince, Maha Thammarcha, but in its weakened state Ayutthaya is vulnerable to a series of invasions by Cambodia.

AMERICAS

EUROPE

AFRICA

WESTERN ASIA

SOUTH & CENTRAL ASIA

EAST ASIA & OCEANIA

1560–1570 A.D.

IVAN THE TERRIBLE

IVAN IV VASILYEVICH WAS THE FIRST RUSSIAN *ruler ever to give himself the title "czar," but history has always known him as "Ivan the Terrible." The name is no exaggeration: In the later years of his reign he was truly terrifying in the unpredictability of his murderous moods and the savage cruelty with which he acted toward his subjects. And yet, for better or for worse, he helped shape the destiny of modern Russia and did much to create the character of his country.*

▲ Shown here in a contemporary woodcut, Ivan was an energetic but unbalanced ruler who became infamous for his impulsive cruelty. Even as a child he had a reputation for torturing small animas and birds.

The people of Novgorod could hardly believe what was happening. They were herded like frightened livestock into city squares. Buildings burned all around as men, women, and children in their thousands were impaled, eviscerated, flayed, or boiled alive. The nature of the "Novgorod Treason" of 1570 for which they were so savagely punished was never entirely clear: The czar may have feared that the northern city meant to secede to neighboring Lithuania, itself recently joined to Poland by the Union of Lublin. Some people, however, suspected that the affluence and sophistication of the prosperous trading center had simply affronted the dour and suspicious czar, who was known to explode into anger at the least provocation.

Born in 1533, Ivan Vasilyevich had begun his apprenticeship in violent intrigue early: He became grand duke of Muscovy at the age of three. Only five years later his mother, the regent, died—probably poisoned—leaving him an orphan to be manipulated by the different factions of boyars (nobles) at the Moscow court. But Ivan had his own ideas and at 13 ordered his first assassination. In 1547 he took power personally, becoming the first Russian ruler to adopt the title "czar" (from the Roman "Caesar"). His marriage to Anastasia Zakharina soon after seems to have stabilized his life to some extent, and he gave up the dissolute pleasures that had marked his youth.

Ivan's reign began promisingly. The young ruler showed a capacity for effective action when in 1552 he conquered the Mongol Khanate of Kazan. The next year, in the aftermath of English navigator Richard Chancellor's discovery of the White Sea route to Russia's north coast, he reopened trade with the West. He extended his kingdom again in 1556, taking the Khanate of Astrakhan and so opening the way to the Volga River, the Caspian Sea, the Caucasus Mountains, and ultimately Siberia. In 1558 he attacked the Germanic Livonian Knights, who restricted Russian access to the Baltic Sea, but this campaign would turn into a protracted war involving Sweden, northern Europe's leading power at the time.

After Anastasia's death in 1560 Ivan's suspicions spiraled out of control. Paranoia became the determining characteristic of his rule. He divided his kingdom into two, the *oprichnina* or area around Moscow, which was under his own control, and the *zemshchina*, which was supposedly run by a boyars' council. In practice Ivan's own 6,000-strong secret police force, the black-hooded *oprichniki*, roamed the *zemshchina* at will, terrorizing the population and

---

👑 **1533** Birth of Ivan Vasilyevich.

👑 **1536** Ivan's father, Vasily III, dies: Ivan becomes grand duke of Muscovy (Moscow) with his mother as regent.

👑 **1538** Ivan's mother is murdered.

👑 **1547** Ivan takes personal power, becoming the first Russian ruler to bear the title "czar."

⚔ **1552** Ivan's forces conquer the Mongol Khanate of Kazan.

✴ **1553** The English explorer Richard Chancellor opens up the trade route around the North Cape of Norway to Russia's White Sea.

👑 **1553** Ivan's infant son Dmitri drowns in a tragic accident.

St. Basil's Cathedral

Standing on the south side of Moscow's Red Square, St. Basil's Cathedral is one of the world's most famous buildings, instantly recognizable around the globe as a symbol of Russia. With its gaudy onion spires, its ornate facades, and its dark interior honeycombed with small chapels, it proclaims Russia's pride in its unique culture and spirituality. The building was planned as a monument to the conquests of Ivan the Terrible, whose relations with the Orthodox church were often strained; the czar resented the church's hold over Russia's peasantry even as he needed its help in shoring up his authority with the people. He needed church support, too, as a spiritual bulwark against the threat of Protestantism and all the political consequences it was having for the kingdoms to the west. Work on St. Basil's began in 1555, but the building was only finally completed in 1679.

pulling in suspects for torture sessions in which Ivan himself sometimes took an eager part. No one was safe: The head of the Russian Orthodox Church was one victim of the terror; another was Ivan's cousin, Prince Vladimir Staritsky. In 1581, in a rage, the czar even murdered his own son, Ivan. He himself died in 1584, leaving behind a Russia that, although comparatively strong and coherent as a nation, was mired in economic backwardness and ruled by fear.

▼ For all the horrors of his reign, Ivan considerably expanded Russian power eastward, opening up new lands for settlement in the last decades of the 16th century.

▲ A contemporary book illustration shows Ivan's marriage to Anastasia Romanovna in 1547.

ARCTIC OCEAN · Novaya Zemlya · Kara Sea · Barents Sea · NORWAY · SWEDEN · Helsingfors · Narva · Pskov · Archangel 1583 · N. Dvina · Ustyug · Yarensk · Obdorsk 1595 · Pechora · Ob · Berezov 1593 · Samoyeds · Surgut 1594 · Ob · Narym 1596 · Voguls · Pelym 1592 · Verkhotyure 1598 · Tobolsk 1587 · Tyumen 1586 · Yenisey · Tver · Yaroslavl · Vyatka · Smolensk · Moscow · Nizhniy Novgorod · Kazan Tatars · Kazan · Orel 1564 · Ufa 1586 · Kirghiz · Irtysh · Kiev · Voronezh 1586 · Saratov 1590 · Samara 1586 · Volga · Ural Cossacks · Dniepr · Don · Tsaritsyn 1589 · Ural · POLAND · KHANATE OF CRIMEA · Don Cossacks · Azov · Astrakhan Tatars · Nogai Tatars · Aral Sea · Kerch · Astrakhan · Black Sea · CAUCASUS MTS. · Caspian Sea · OTTOMAN EMPIRE

☐ new Russian town with date of foundation
▨ Russia at the accession of Ivan IV 1533
▨ Russian gains under Ivan IV and Fyodor, 1533–98

0 — 800 km
0 — 500 mi

☀ **1555** Construction of St. Basil's Cathedral, Moscow, begins.

✕ **1556** Ivan's forces conquer Astrakhan.

✕ **1558** Eager to gain access to the Baltic Sea, Ivan launches the first of a series of wars against Livonia that will stretch on for 25 years.

🏛 **1560** Ivan's wife Anastasia dies.

🏛 **1569** The Union of Lublin unites Lithuania with Poland.

✕ **1570** Ivan punishes the "Novgorod Treason" by launching a reign of terror in the city.

🏛 **1581** The czar murders his second son, Ivan.

🏛 **1584** Death of Ivan the Terrible. He is succeeded by his third son, Fyodor.

1570–1580 A.D.

AMERICAS

The *Popol Vuh*, some of whose characters are shown on this vase, is the main surviving Mayan literary work. It preserves the creation myths of the Quiché Maya, recounting the struggle of a monstrous bird deity known as Seven Macaw against two heroes, the twins Hunahpu and Xbalanque (seen here hunting waterfowl), in the time before the emergence of the first humans.

📖 **c.1570** The *Popol Vuh*, a compilation of Mayan myths, is written down in the Mayan language by scribes using the Roman alphabet.

EUROPE

⚔ **1571** An army of Crimean Tatars sacks Moscow.

⚔ **1571** A Christian fleet led by Don John of Austria defeats a large Ottoman fleet at the Battle of Lepanto, just off the coast of Greece.

⚔ **1572** The Dutch War of Independence gathers pace with a revolt against the Duke of Alba, the Spanish governor of the Netherlands (–1609).

☀ **1572** Over 2,500 leading Huguenots are slaughtered in Paris during the Massacre of St. Bartholomew's Day.

⚙ **1572** The Danish astronomer Tycho Brahe observes a supernova marking the birth of a new star (now known as Tycho's Star), disproving Aristotle's notion that the heavens are unchanging.

📖 **1572** The Portuguese poet Luis de Camoes publishes *The Lusiads*, Portugal's national epic.

AFRICA

👑 **1570** Under Idris III Aloma, the Saharan Kingdom of Kanem Bornu begins to expand its power.

⚔ **c.1572** The king of Kongo drives out the Jaga invaders who had laid waste to his country.

⚙ **1572** An epidemic in Algiers kills one third of the population.

WESTERN ASIA

⚔ **1570** The Ottoman Empire declares war on Venice and invades Cyprus.

👑 **1574** Murad III becomes Ottoman sultan.

👑 **1576** Shah Tahmasp I of Persia dies; his son succeeds him as Esmail II but reigns for less than a year.

SOUTH & CENTRAL ASIA

⚔ **1574** The Mughals conquer Gujarat, giving them access to the Indian Ocean.

☀ **1576** The first annual pilgrimage caravan sets out from India to the Muslim holy cities of Mecca and Medina, paid for and organized by the Mughal Emperor Akbar.

⚔ **1576** The Mughals conquer Bengal from the Afghans, extending their rule across the whole of northern India.

EAST ASIA & OCEANIA

⚙ **1570** The port of Nagasaki in Japan is opened to foreign trade.

⚙ **1571** The Spanish found Manila on the island of Luzon (Philippines).

👑 **1573** Oda Nobunaga drives the Ashikaga shogun out of Kyoto, ending the Ashikaga Shogunate.

👑 **1573** Accession of Wan-li as emperor of China; his reign is a time of great unrest.

This gilded copper statue represents Sonam Gyatso, the third Dalai Lama of Tibet.

⊕ **c.1575** The Dominican friar Bernardino de Sahagún compiles an illustrated account of Aztec myths, history, and customs, based on firsthand accounts from native informants.

⊕ **1576** The English mariner Martin Frobisher explores the Labrador coast and Baffin Island, discovering and naming Frobisher Bay (–1578).

⊕ **1578** English seaman Francis Drake raids Spanish bullion ships off the Pacific coast of South and Central America.

⊕ **1579** Drake claims land near modern San Francisco and names it New Albion.

👑 **1574** Henry III becomes king of France on the death of his brother, Charles IX.

📖 **1575** The Greek painter Domenikos Theotokopoulos settles in Toledo, Spain, where he achieves fame as El Greco ("the Greek").

✕ **1576** In response to the Dutch revolt Spanish troops sack the city of Antwerp in the Netherlands, killing 7,000 people.

The victory of a Christian fleet over the Ottoman navy at the Battle of Lepanto revived Western morale after a string of defeats.

👑 **1576** Rudolf II of Hungary becomes Holy Roman emperor; his court at Prague is a center for writers, artists, and humanist scholars.

📖 **1577** Death of the Venetian-born painter Titian, court painter to Charles V and Philip II of Spain and the greatest artist of the late Renaissance.

👑 **1579** The seven rebel provinces of the Netherlands form the Union of Utrecht under the leadership of William the Silent.

👑 **1574** The Ottomans fight off an attempt by Christian forces to retake Tunis.

⊕ **1575** The Portuguese found a base at Luanda in Angola that becomes a center of the slave trade.

✕ **1578** The Moroccans defeat and kill King Sebastian I of Portugal at the Battle of Kasr al-Kabir.

✕ **1578** Murad III launches a war against Safavid Persia.

Amritsar in the Punjab region of northern India was founded as a holy city by Ram Das, fourth guru (spiritual leader) of the Sikh faith, around a sacred pool, the Amrita Saras. Its most famous building, the Golden Temple, stands on an island in the lake. It owes its name to a covering of gold leaf added in the early 19th century.

☀ **1577** Amritsar is founded as a holy city of the Sikhs in the Punjab.

👑 **1579** Akbar abolishes the *jiziya*, an annual property tax levied on non-Muslim subjects.

⊕ **1575** A Spanish expedition from Manila visits Canton, South China, in an attempt to gain trading privileges.

⊕ **1576** Oda Nobunaga constructs a mighty fortress at Azuchi, initiating a period of castle building in Japan.

☀ **c.1577** Altan Khan, ruler of the Tumed Mongols, adopts Buddhism and recognizes the spiritual authority of the Tibetan monk Sonam Gyatso, giving him the name of Dalai Lama ("Ocean of Wisdom"). Sonam is taken as the third incarnation of the Dalai Lama.

✕ **1577** Hideyoshi, Oda Nobunaga's general, begins the conquest of western Japan.

⊕ **1578** Chinese scholar Li Shih-Shen completes the *Great Pharmacopoeia*, in which he describes more than 2,000 drugs.

AMERICAS

EUROPE

AFRICA

WESTERN ASIA

SOUTH & CENTRAL ASIA

EAST ASIA & OCEANIA

1570–1580 A.D.

INDIA'S MUGHAL EMPIRE

▲ The splendor of the Mughal emperors was captured in the works of a brilliant school of miniature painters. Here Humayun is shown holding a falcon.

THE MUGHAL DYNASTY RULED *most of India and Pakistan for more than 200 years. Theirs was one of three great Muslim empires that dominated western and southern Asia at this time, the others being the Ottoman Empire in West Asia and the Safavid Empire in Persia. The Mughals are remembered today for their rich legacy of Islamic art and architecture as well as for their administrative efficiency and stable government, which united Muslims and Hindus in a single state.*

The founder of the Mughal Dynasty was Babur, who claimed descent from Timur and Genghis Khan, the great Mongol leaders of the past—Mughal (sometimes spelled Mogul) is the Arabic form of Mongol. Babur was the hereditary prince of Ferghana in Central Asia but was driven out of his lands by the Uzbeks. Inspired as a boy by tales of the deeds of his ancestors, he sought adventure and conquest on the battlefield and by 1504 had made himself ruler of Kabul in Afghanistan. From there he turned his attention to India. In 1526 Babur swept down into the Ganges Plain at the head of an army of 12,000 men. His soldiers, equipped with cannons and firearms, defeated the last sultan of Delhi at the Battle of Panipat, and by the time of his death in 1530 Babur had conquered most of northern India.

Babur's empire was all but lost during the reign of his son Humayun. Afghan rebels took over most of

the Mughal territory in northern India, and Humayun himself was forced into exile for a time. It was Babur's grandson Akbar (reigned 1555–1605) who established the true greatness of the Mughal Empire. He was almost constantly at war and not only won back Babur's empire but also extended Mughal rule across the whole of northern India and into the Deccan Plateau. Although he did not hesitate to punish his enemies with brutal force when necessary, Akbar gave the Mughal Empire stability and a strong system of government by pursuing tolerant policies toward his Hindu subjects. He married the daughter of the Hindu ruler of Amber and, although he never renounced Islam, encouraged debate with other religions and even celebrated some of the major Hindu festivals at his court.

There were three more outstanding Mughal emperors after Akbar. Under Jahangir's tolerant rule

Mughal Architecture

The Mughals were descended from the nomadic Mongol rulers of Central Asia, whose courts were movable tented cities, complete with palaces and bazaars. The Mughal court, which was also the administrative capital of the empire, rarely remained in one place for long, regularly shifting between Agra and Delhi. The Mughal emperors were prolific builders and endowed their capitals with edifices in brick, marble, and stone. In 1570 Akbar took the unusual step of constructing a new capital from scratch. He named it Fatehpur Sikri ("City of Victory") but occupied it for less than 15 years before moving the capital to Lahore to cope with unrest in neighboring Afghanistan. Never reoccupied, Fatehpur Sikri today contains some of the finest examples of Islamic architecture in India, especially the Jami Mosque and the Diwan-i Khass, or audience hall, which lay at the heart of Akbar's palace complex.

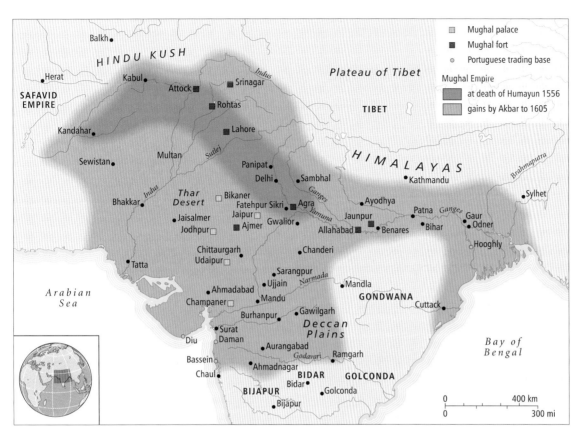

◀ The Mughal Empire in India was founded by Babur and partly lost by his heir Humayun. Its third ruler, Akbar, carried Mughal power across the subcontinent to the east coast and southward through land contolled by the various Rajput dynasties onto the central plateau known as the Deccan. In the 17th century Aurangzeb would extend its boundaries even farther into the deep south.

from 1605 to 1627 Mughal arts flourished, and miniature painting reached rare heights. In the reign of the next emperor, Shah Jahan (1628–58), the influence of Islam grew much stronger. The empire reached its greatest extent under Aurangzeb (1658–1707); but although it remained outwardly strong and prosperous, Aurangzeb's increasingly harsh treatment of Hindus caused rebellions in many parts of the country. Mughal power weakened rapidly after his death, and the empire began to break up. By 1748 the Mughals ruled only the area around Delhi, and in 1857 they passed out of history.

🎓 **1483** Birth of Babur in Ferghana, Central Asia.

🎓 **1504** Babur takes possession of Kabul, Afghanistan.

✕ **1526** Babur defeats Sultan Ibrahim Lodi at the Battle of Panipat, north of Delhi, and founds the Mughal Empire.

🎓 **1530** Death of Babur; he is succeeded by Humayun.

🎓 **1540** Humayun loses northern India to Afghan rebels and goes into exile in Persia.

🎓 **1555** Humayun recaptures Delhi; he dies soon after and is succeeded by his son Akbar, aged 13.

✕ **1556** Akbar's army defeats Hemu, a Hindu usurper, at the second Battle of Panipat.

✕ **1568** Akbar captures the Rajput fortress of Chittor, which is holding out against him, and massacres all its inhabitants.

🎓 **1570** Akbar builds and occupies a new capital at Fatehpur Sikri (–1584).

☀ **1580** Three Jesuit priests from Goa visit Fatehpur Sikri at Akbar's invitation to debate religion with him.

🎓 **1605** Akbar dies: Salim, Akbar's son, becomes emperor, taking the name of Jahangir.

📖 **1618** Abu'l Hasan, the greatest of the Mughal miniature painters, is given the title of *Nadiru-zaman* ("Wonder of the Age") by Jahangir.

🎓 **1627** On the death of Jahangir his son Khurram murders his brothers and nephews to ensure his succession as emperor (in 1628); he rules as Shah Jahan.

📖 **1638** Shah Jahan builds India's best-known building, the Taj Mahal, as a memorial to his wife, Mumtaz Mahal.

🎓 **1658** Aurangzeb, the last of the great Moghul emperors, comes to the throne; he will reign to 1707.

AMERICAS

1583 Sir Humphrey Gilbert founds the first English colony in North America at what is now St. John's, Newfoundland.

1584 Walter Raleigh founds an English colony on Roanoke Island off the coast of Virginia, but it is quickly abandoned (–1585).

The scant remains of an earthen fort are all that survives of the colony on Roanoke Island.

1585 English navigator John Davis undertakes three Arctic voyages in search of the northwest passage; the Davis Strait between Greenland and Baffin Island is named for him (–1587).

EUROPE

1580 After defeating a Portuguese army at the Battle of Alcantara, Philip II of Spain claims the throne of Portugal.

1582 The Gregorian calendar, introduced by Pope Gregory XIII for whom it is named, replaces the Julian calendar. The new calendar is accepted at once by most Catholic countries but only gradually by Protestant ones.

1584 The port of Archangel is founded on the White Sea, giving Russia limited access to the ocean. (It is only open in the summer months since it lies within the Arctic Circle).

AFRICA

c.1580 Idris III Aloma buys firearms from the Ottoman Empire to strengthen his hold over the trade routes of the eastern Sahara.

1581 The Moroccans under Ahmed al-Mansur of the Sharifian Dynasty occupy Tuat in the northern Sahara.

c.1585 The Portuguese wage a series of military campaigns against local rulers in Angola and force them to accept their rule in return for a share in the slave trade.

WESTERN ASIA

c.1580 The Ottomans' *devshirme* system of recruiting Christian boys for the Janissaries, the sultan's crack troops, goes into decline under Murad III.

1582 Murad III, who is known for his love of display, gives a festival in Istanbul to celebrate his son's circumcision, with banquets and mock battles; it lasts for 55 days.

1583 The Ottomans take the city of Baku on the west coast of the Caspian Sea from the Safavid rulers of Persia.

SOUTH & CENTRAL ASIA

c. 1580 The Mughal Emperor Akbar brings together Hindu and Persian scholars to translate the Hindu religious epic, the *Mahabharata*, into Persian.

1582 Akbar sets out the Din-I Ilahi (Divine Faith); it incorporates ideas from other Asian religions, including Jainism and Hinduism, as well as Islam.

EAST ASIA & OCEANIA

1582 In Japan Oda Nobunaga is assassinated, and his general Hideyoshi seizes power.

1582 Ming Emperor Wan-li refuses to conduct court business, and power passes into the hands of the royal eunuchs.

Hideyoshi (1536–1598) was the only man of peasant birth to rule Japan. Rising through the ranks in the service of Oda Nobunaga, he staged a coup on Nobunaga's death, having himself made *kanpaku* (civil regent) by the emperor. He then forced the *daimyo* (feudal lords) into line and disarmed the peasants. In his later years he staged a futile attempt to conquer Korea that cost many lives and almost bankrupted the state.

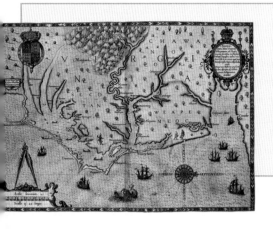

Seen in a 17th-century map, Roanoke Island off the North Carolina coast was the site of the first English colony in the future United States, promoted by the explorer Walter Raleigh. The first attempt, in 1584, failed, with the survivors returning to England. The second three years later simply vanished; no trace of the colonists could be found when help finally came in 1591.

⊕ **1585** The first recorded commercial shipment of chocolate is sent from Veracruz, Mexico, to Spain.

⊕ **1587** Governor John White lands a party of 117 settlers on Roanoke Island in a second attempt to found a colony there.

🏛 **1584** Boris Godunov, a nobleman of nonroyal birth, becomes virtual ruler of Russia on the death of Ivan IV and the succession of his feeble son Fyodor.

🏛 **1584** Death of William the Silent, leader of the Dutch revolt against Spain.

🏛 **1589** Henry of Navarre, a Protestant, becomes the first of the Bourbon kings of France as King Henry IV.

✕ **1589** Philip II of Spain declares war on France in support of the Catholics opposed to Henry IV.

⊕ **1588** The English Guinea Company is founded to trade with West Africa.

🏛 **1588** Abbas I becomes shah of Persia; he will become the greatest of the Safavid rulers, famed for his patronage of the arts, especially miniature painting.

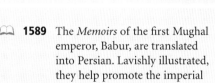

A miniature painting shows young noblemen serving food and drink to Persia's Shah Abbas.

🏛 **1585** Akbar moves his capital to Lahore in Punjab.

📖 **1589** The *Memoirs* of the first Mughal emperor, Babur, are translated into Persian. Lavishly illustrated, they help promote the imperial image of the Mughal Dynasty.

☀ **1583** The Jesuit priest Father Matteo Ricci arrives in Macao as the first Christian missionary to China.

🏛 **1583** As a sign of his supremacy over central Japan, Hideyoshi begins to construct a great castle at Osaka.

🏛 **1585** The Sultan of Aceh (Indonesia) sends a diplomatic letter to England's Queen Elizabeth.

🏛 **1587** Hideyoshi orders the expulsion of Jesuit missionaries from Japan and takes control of the port of Nagasaki.

🏛 **1587** Hideyoshi demonstrates his power over the Japanese court by hosting a lavish 10-day tea ceremony attended by Emperor Go-Yozei.

AMERICAS

EUROPE

AFRICA

WESTERN ASIA

SOUTH & CENTRAL ASIA

EAST ASIA & OCEANIA

1580–1590 A.D.

ELIZABETH'S ENGLAND

LATER GENERATIONS LOOKED BACK *on the reign of England's Queen Elizabeth I as a golden age, the time of "Merrie England." To her subjects she was "Good Queen Bess." During her long reign of nearly 50 years England was transformed from a divided country troubled by religious strife to one of comparative peace, stability, and prosperity, an outcome that owed much to Elizabeth's determination and strength of character.*

▲ Queen Elizabeth watched over her public image as carefully as any modern politician. This portrait of the ruler in all her finery was painted by Nicholas Hilliard in 1575, when she was 42 years of age.

Born in 1533, Elizabeth was the daughter of King Henry VIII and his second wife, Anne Boleyn. Henry already had a daughter, Mary, by his first wife, Catherine of Aragon, but he desperately wanted a son. In order to divorce Catherine and marry Anne, Henry split with the Roman Catholic church and declared himself head of the newly created Church of England, displacing the pope. But Anne's failure to produce a son led to her downfall, and less than three years after Elizabeth's birth she was executed on the king's orders. Although the young princess rarely saw her father after that, she received the education usually reserved for the male heirs of Renaissance monarchs and was instructed in Greek, Latin, history, philosophy, and theology as well as French and Italian. She proved an intelligent and eager scholar.

Henry died in 1547 and was succeeded by his 10-year-old son Edward VI, the son of his third wife, Jane Seymour. Although young, Edward held strong

William Shakespeare

William Shakespeare, the greatest writer of the Elizabethan age, was born in 1564 in the small country town of Stratford-on-Avon. By the early 1590s he was living in London, where he became a member of the Lord Chamberlain's Men, a company of actors paid for by Queen Elizabeth. He soon found fame as the author of a stream of plays—comedies, histories, romances, and tragedies—that won him popular acclaim and favor at court. His use of language was unsurpassed, and his words, expressions, and characters have entered the English language and imagination. He died in Stratford in 1616.

◄ Elizabeth's onetime brother-in-law, Philip II of Spain, sent an armada (fleet) of 130 ships to invade her kingdom in 1588. The boats headed for the Spanish Netherlands, planning to take on extra troops, but their formation was wrecked by English fireships. Cutting anchor, the boats were swept north by a storm that completed the havoc the English warships had begun. Barely half the fleet eventually made its way back to Spain.

Protestant views, and the Reformation flourished in England. But when Edward died suddenly at the age of 16, his eldest half-sister, Mary, a devout Roman Catholic, became queen. Determined that England should become Catholic again, Mary had many Protestants burned at the stake. These were unhappy years for Elizabeth; and when she found herself queen on the death of Mary in 1558, she was already well skilled in the arts of political survival.

Her harsh early lessons in life served Elizabeth well. From the beginning she ruled wisely and strongly, kept her own counsel, chose her advisers carefully, and maintained good relations with Parliament. One of her first moves was to restore Protestantism in England, but she baulked at the extreme measures employed both by her brother Edward and by Mary to force religious change on her subjects, believing that England needed a period of stability and calm to recover from the religious and political upheavals of the recent past.

Many people thought it unnatural for a woman to rule over men, but Elizabeth did not consider herself inferior to any man, nor, as queen, would she submit to any man's authority. She never married but instead built up a strong personal cult, surrounding herself with courtiers, poets, and painters who celebrated her image as the Virgin Queen. Her reign was a time of expansion for England: Sir Francis Drake, Sir John Hawkins, and Sir Walter Raleigh, among other English adventurers, helped make the country rich through exploration, trade, and plunder. Their exploits overseas, especially against the power of Spain, added to the newfound sense of national pride that Elizabeth's long reign helped forge.

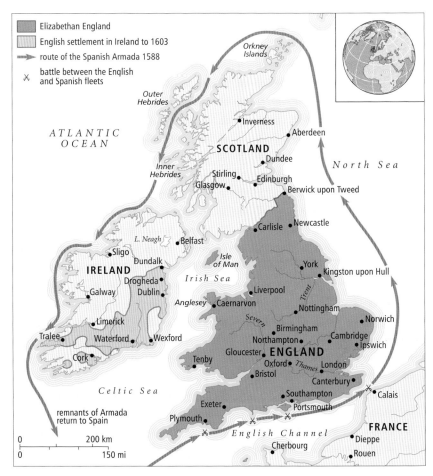

▲ The naval battles against the Armada in 1588 all took place along England's south coast. Thereafter storms swept the remnants of the Spanish fleet around Scotland and Ireland.

👑 **1533** Elizabeth is born at Greenwich Palace, near London.

👑 **1536** Elizabeth's mother, Anne Boleyn, is executed on charges of treason and adultery.

👑 **1549** Thomas Seymour, lord high admiral of England and Elizabeth's guardian, is accused of plotting to marry Elizabeth and beheaded for treason.

👑 **1554** Queen Mary suspects Elizabeth of treason and holds her prisoner.

👑 **1558** On the death of Mary Elizabeth is crowned queen of England.

☀ **1559** Parliament declares Elizabeth supreme governor of the Church of England and restores the use of the English Prayer Book.

⊕ **1562** Elizabeth nearly dies of smallpox.

✕ **1585** Elizabeth sends an army led by the earl of Leicester to the Netherlands to support the Protestant revolt against Spain.

👑 **1587** Mary, queen of Scots, Elizabeth's cousin and an exile in England, is found guilty of plotting to murder Queen Elizabeth and is executed.

✕ **1588** King Philip II of Spain sends the Armada, a fleet of 130 warships, to invade England.

📖 **1590** Edmund Spenser publishes the first three books of *The Faerie Queene*, a narrative poem written in celebration of Queen Elizabeth.

📖 **1598** The Globe Theater in London opens with a performance of William Shakespeare's *Henry V*.

👑 **1601** Robert Devereux, earl of Essex, the queen's former favorite, leads a rebellion against her; he is executed for treason.

👑 **1603** Elizabeth dies and is succeeded by James VI of Scotland, son of Mary, queen of Scots.

AMERICAS

⚙ **1591** John White, governor of Roanoke Island, returns with supplies for the struggling colony but finds it abandoned.

⚙ **1595** The English courtier and adventurer Walter Raleigh explores the coast of Trinidad and sails up the Orinoco River.

⚔ **1595** The English buccaneer Francis Drake tries unsuccessfully to sack Panama, the commercial heart of Spain's overseas empire.

EUROPE

⚙ **c.1590** John Harington, a courtier to Queen Elizabeth, invents the flush toilet and installs one in her palace at Richmond.

⚕ **1592** Sigismund, king of Poland since 1587, succeeds his brother John III as king of Sweden; his attempts to restore Catholicism lead to a rebellion, and he is deposed (–1599).

⚔ **1593** Henry IV brings the French wars of religion to an end by renouncing his Protestant faith and winning the acceptance of his Catholic subjects (–1598).

⚔ **1594** Hugh O'Neill, earl of Tyrone, leads a rebellion in Ireland against English rule.

⚙ **c.1595** The telescope is invented in the Netherlands.

⚕ **1596** The Spanish crown is bankrupt, and the country's population falls as a result of several years of famine and plague.

☀ **1598** Henry IV signs the Edict of Nantes, guaranteeing religious toleration in France.

An astronomer searches the sky with the aid of an early telescope.

AFRICA

⚔ **1590** The Moroccans mount a military expedition across the Sahara to overthrow the once-powerful Songhai Empire, now in decline (–1591).

⚔ **1593** The Portuguese build Fort Jesus just outside Mombasa on Africa's east coast and sack the long-established Islamic trading port.

WESTERN ASIA

⚕ **1590** The Ottoman and Safavid empires make peace, fixing their frontier at the Caspian Sea.

Shah Nematollah's Tomb, Mahan, Iran, built on the orders of Shah Abbas.

SOUTH & CENTRAL ASIA

⚕ **1591** The sultan of Golconda, one of the principal Muslim rulers of India's Deccan Plateau, founds a new city at Hyderabad on the Musi River in what is now Andhra Pradesh.

⚔ **1595** Emperor Akbar's forces capture Kandahar, bringing Afghanistan under Mughal control.

⚕ **1598** With the northwest pacified, Akbar moves his capital to Agra.

EAST ASIA & OCEANIA

⚕ **1591** Hideyoshi conquers the northern part of Honshu Island, effectively reuniting Japan.

⚔ **1592** Hideyoshi invades Korea with the ultimate aim of attacking China, but the strength of the Korean navy forces him to retreat.

⚕ **1592** The Ming court sends military aid to Korea.

📖 **1592** Wu Che'eng-en publishes *Monkey*, a classic Chinese novel.

☀ **1595** Matteo Ricci adopts the dress of a Confucian scholar and makes a first unsuccessful attempt to enter the Imperial City in Beijing; he then settles in Nanking.

⚙ **1595** Cornelis Houtman leads the first Dutch trading expedition to the Spice Islands (Indonesia).

⚔ **1596** The Japanese invade Korea for a second time, but an organized defense by combined Chinese and Korean forces halts their advance.

⚙ **1597** Houtman's expedition visits Bali before returning home.

⊛ **1598** The Marquis de la Roche founds a short-lived French colony on Sable Island, off the coast of Nova Scotia (–1603).

⊛ **1598** Spanish settlers prospecting for precious metals occupy San Juan Pueblo in the Rio Grande Valley of what is now New Mexico.

A favorite of Ivan the Terrible, Boris Godunov served on his death as regent for the czar's young heir Fyodor. As the true ruler of Russia at this time, he provided capable leadership, winning back land earlier lost to Sweden and encouraging the colonization of Siberia. When Fyodor died in 1598 without leaving an heir, Boris was chosen by a popular assembly to be czar. In contrast to the success of the regency, his short reign was beset by unrest, caused largely by a devastating three-year famine. Usurpers arose to challenge the legitimacy of his rule, and on his death in 1605 the nation was plunged into ten years of anarchy, the Time of Troubles.

👑 **1598** Boris Godunov is elected czar of Russia on the death of Fyodor.

✕ **1598** With the Treaty of Vervins Philip II of Spain ends the war with France.

👑 **1598** Death of Philip II; he is succeeded by his son Philip III.

👑 **1594** The Portuguese have by now established control over most of coastal Angola but are unable to penetrate far into the interior because of disease.

⊛ **1596** Dutch traders are present in Guinea on the West African coast.

⊛ **1596** The Dutch establish a trading base on the island of Mauritius in the Indian Ocean.

👑 **1595** On becoming Ottoman sultan, Mehmed III murders 20 of his younger brothers to prevent them setting up as rivals for his throne.

📖 **1597** Shah Abbas of Persia moves the Safavid capital to Esfahan, where he builds a new city adorned with many fine buildings.

✕ **1597** The Safavids win a major victory over the Uzbeks, halting their incursions into Khurasan in northeast Persia.

☀ **1599** The Portuguese archbishop of Goa calls a synod at Diamper at which the Syrian Church of Kerala (in southern India) is formally united with the Roman Catholic church.

👑 **1598** Hideyoshi dies suddenly, and the invasion of Korea is abandoned; many Korean craftsmen are forcibly transported to Japan.

Cornelis Houtman's fleet returns to Amsterdam, as shown in a 17th-century Dutch painting.

1590–1600 A.D.

AMERICAS

EUROPE

AFRICA

WESTERN ASIA

SOUTH & CENTRAL ASIA

EAST ASIA & OCEANIA

THE GUNPOWDER REVOLUTION

BY THE END OF THE 16TH CENTURY *the gunpowder revolution had finally come of age. By that time armies in Europe and Asia had been using gunpowder-fired weapons for nearly 300 years, and guns, which had at first been little more than military curiosities, had become the main battlefield weapon, transforming the way that war was waged. But the gunpowder revolution altered more than just the face of combat. It stimulated closer study of chemistry, mathematics, and mechanics, and brought about important advances in metal casting, so paving the way for the development of modern science. Unexpectedly, it also increased the power of the state.*

▲ An Italian engraving shows a metalworker casting a section of a cannon in a forge. Heavy artillery was costly to produce, making it difficult for the private forces of individual nobles to compete against the armies of the state.

Gunpowder is a mixture of potassium nitrate (saltpeter), charcoal, and sulfur. When lit, it explodes with enough force to propel a missile along a barrel or tube. The Chinese knew about the explosive properties of gunpowder as early as the 1st century A.D. At first they seem to have used it only to set off firecrackers at religious ceremonies, but by the 10th century they were employing it on the battlefield to shoot fire-arrows down bamboo tubes. News of this startling technology reached Europe early in the 13th century, after Chinese troops used gunpowder-fired rockets in their wars against the Mongols.

It was in Europe that the first cannons were developed. Short tubes of bronze or iron firing stone balls, they proved useful in siege warfare. However, they often exploded while being fired, killing the gunners, and it is doubtful how much damage they actually caused, although the noise and smoke of the explosion must have terrified the enemy.

Over the next two centuries weapon technology and design steadily improved. Metalworkers developed alloys of bronze and iron capable of withstanding the shock of the explosion. Trunnions (lugs) were fixed to the barrel so that the gunners could adjust the angle of fire. Cannons became steadily smaller and lighter, while the addition of

✹ **1232**	First recorded use of gunpowder-fired rockets by the Chinese against a Mongol army.	✕ **1420**	Small artillery pieces and handguns are used during the Hussite Wars in the Czech lands (−1433).
✹ **1248**	An Oxford scholar, Roger Bacon, makes the first-known reference to gunpowder in Europe.	✕ **1449**	Mons Meg, a giant iron bombard (cannon), is made for Philip the Good, duke of Burgundy.
✕ **1331**	Cannons are used at the siege of Cividale, Italy.	✕ **1450**	The French use two culverins—long-barreled cannons—against English longbowmen at the Battle of Formigny.
✹ **1376**	Reference is made to a cannon foundry at Venice.		
✕ **1389**	The Turks use cannons at the siege of Kosovo.	✕ **1454**	The French develop the two-wheeled gun carriage.
✹ **1411**	First-known manuscript illustration of a matchlock trigger mechanism.	✕ **c.1525**	By this time the shoulder stock is in use on small arms.

▶ A book illustration dated to 1512 shows various models of harquebus, the predecessor of the musket. At first it took two people to fire the gun—one to hold and aim it and another to light the fuse, as shown here. Later, the invention of the matchlock—a pivoting fuse that could be lowered with a flick of the thumb to ignite the charge of gunpowder—made it possible for a single person to aim and fire. In the early days supports were often used to steady the gun and bear the weight of the long barrel.

wheeled carriages gave them greater mobility. Finally, more efficient mixtures of gunpowder were found.

By the middle of the 15th century the first small arms were appearing on the battlefield. At first, one gunner held a small hand cannon fastened to a simple wooden stock braced against his arm, while a second person fired it. Then a pivoting firing mechanism called a matchlock was attached to the stock, making it possible for a single person to aim and fire the gun by squeezing a trigger. Arms of this sort were first developed in Germany and were called harquebuses. Their use spread rapidly throughout Europe and the Ottoman Empire. By the 16th century harquebuses had developed into muskets, comparatively accurate weapons that could kill a man at 300 paces. At the same time, powerful cannons had been place on board ships, transforming naval warfare.

One unexpected consequence of the revolution was to increase the power of rulers. Producing field artillery and arming infantry regiments with muskets were too expensive for even great lords to afford, so private armies fell into disuse. By the end of the 16th century guns and gunpowder were made under royal license, and armies and arsenals were maintained at the expense of the government. Large-scale warfare had become the monopoly of the state.

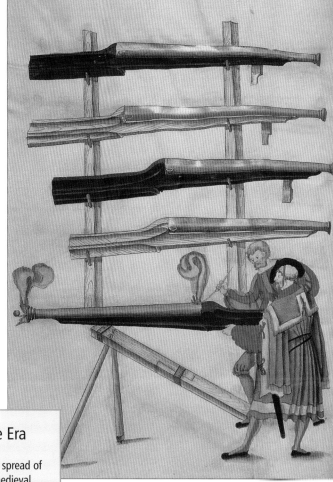

The End of the Castle Era

One of the main results of the spread of guns was the decline of the medieval castle. The fall of Constantinople to the bombardment of Ottoman siege artillery in 1453 showed that high stone walls and tall flanking towers were no defense against siege cannons. To counter the threat, military engineers were soon experimenting with new ways of constructing fortifications. As at England's Deal Castle (left), walls and towers were sunk behind a ditch and faced with a stone parapet. Beyond the ditch a sloping earthen bank, or glacis, exposed the attackers to cannon and harquebus fire from the parapet, while also serving to bounce incoming cannonballs harmlessly over the defenders on the walls. Rounded or pointed bastions projected out into the ditch to provide gun platforms to give flanking fire. The first bastioned fortresses of this kind were built in northern Italy to designs drawn up by artist–engineers such as Leonardo da Vinci and Francesco di Giorgio.

✕ **1527** Venetian galleys are equipped with lidded gunports.

⊕ **1537** Ligatures (stitches) are first used to treat gunshot wounds.

⊕ **1543** The English perfect an improved method for casting iron cannons.

✕ **c.1550** The musket replaces the crossbow as the main battlefield weapon (other than swords) in Europe.

✕ **1588** The Armada sees the first artillery battle between massed warships at sea.

FACTS AT A GLANCE

absolutism
A system of government in which the authority of the ruler is total, with no one to account to and no restraining checks and balances.

Aceh
Northeastern region of the island of Sumatra in Indonesia. The first Muslim stronghold in Southeast Asia, it reached a political zenith under Sultan Iskander Muda (1607–1636). Aceh fiercely resisted Portuguese and later Dutch intervention.

Aden
A seaport in the far southwest of the Arabian Peninsula, since early times a center for Indian Ocean trade. In the 1540s an Ottoman garrison and naval base were established there to resist Portuguese expansion in the region.

Ahmad Gran
Muslim imam and ruler of Adal, in southern Eritrea, from 1507. Ahmad Gran expanded its territories steadily inland into Ethiopia until his defeat and death at the hands of a combined Ethiopian–Portuguese force in 1543.

Alba, Duke of
Spanish general (1507–1582) who was given the task of restoring control in the Netherlands by King Philip II of Spain and set up a reign of terror there; his name is sometimes given as Alva.

alchemy
Medieval pseudoscience that claimed to be able to transform base metals into precious metals, notably gold; it was supplanted by the rise of the science of chemistry in the 18th century.

Anabaptists
Members of a radical Protestant sect in Germany who believed in adult baptism and the complete separation of church and state; they were frequently persecuted for their extreme views.

Anatolia
The Asiatic part of Turkey, known in Roman times as Asia Minor.

Angkor
The ancient capital of the Khmer Empire in northwestern Cambodia, whose ruins date mainly from the 10th to 12th centuries. Angkor Wat, the greatest of its Hindu temples, was built in the early 12th century.

Anglican
Anything relating to the Church of England or a member of that church.

Aragon
Northern region of Spain. An independent kingdom in medieval times, it was united with Castile in 1469 when its king, Ferdinand II, married Isabella of Castile; their joint realm became the foundation of a united Spain.

archbishopric
The center of an ecclesiastical province in the Christian church, presided over by an archbishop.

Archbishop of Canterbury
The highest-ranking English bishop who, after the split with the papacy in the 16th century, became the head of the independent Anglican church.

Armada
The Spanish word for a military fleet. Specifically, it refers to the fleet of 130 warships carrying almost 20,000 soldiers sent by Philip II of Spain in 1588 to invade England.

Aristotle
Greek philosopher and scientist (384–322 B.C.) who became tutor to Alexander the Great in 342. On returning to Athens, he set up his own school at the Lyceum.

Ashikaga Shogunate
Period of Japanese history from 1336 to 1573 when the Ashikaga family held the office of shogun (military governor).

Astrakhan, Khanate of
A realm on the lower Volga River in Central Asia that was originally part of the empire of the Golden Horde but broke away to become an independent khanate until its conquest by Czar Ivan the Terrible of Russia from 1554 to 1556.

audiencia
In Spanish America a tribunal responsible to the Spanish crown that first supervised and then supplanted the authority of the conquistadors in governing the newly conquered territories.

Ayutthaya
Thai kingdom that rose to prominence in about 1350. After the capture of Angkor in 1431 Ayutthaya also ruled much of Cambodia. The realm was destroyed by the Burmese in 1767.

Aztecs
Mesoamerican people who built an empire centered on the Valley of Mexico in the course of the 15th century. Their origins are uncertain; they are believed to have moved into the valley from the north, probably around the year 1200. They built their capital, Tenochtitlán, on the site of present-day Mexico City.

Banten
Also known as Bantam. Muslim sultanate in western Java, Indonesia. Its capital of the same name was an important trading center attracting Dutch and English merchants.

Barbarossa
Latin for "Redbeard," the nickname given to two brothers, Uruj and Khayr ad-din (or Hayreddin), both corsairs preying on the shipping of Christian Europe. After Uruj's death in 1519 Khayr ad-din sought the protection of Sultan Selim I, but remained the effective ruler of Tunis and Algiers.

Barbary States
Nominally provinces of the Ottoman Empire, these states in what are now Libya, Tunisia, Algeria, and Morocco were ruled by the Barbarossa brothers and by successive generations of corsairs.

bastion
A projecting part of a fortification, built out from the wall.

Bengal
Region in northeastern India. Ruled from ancient times by Buddhist dynasties, it later became an independent Muslim kingdom under Afghan rule before its annexation by the Mughal Empire in 1576. After the British founded Calcutta, Bengal came under the control of their East India Company. It is now divided between the Indian state of West Bengal and Bangladesh.

Bidar
Now located in the southern Indian state of Karnataka, Bidar was originally the capital of the Bahmani Kingdom. Under the Barid Shahi Dynasty it was the home of one of the five Muslim Deccani Sultanates until its annexation by the Mughals in 1657.

Bourbon Dynasty
The line of French kings founded by King Henry IV (ruled 1589–1610). The Bourbons were deposed during the French Revolution but restored to the throne in 1814. The last Bourbon king of France was Louis Philippe (reigned 1830–1848).

boyar
A member of the landowning group of Russian aristocrats whose power was broken by Czar Ivan the Terrible in 1565.

buccaneer
An English, Dutch, or French adventurer who preyed on Spanish shipping in the Caribbean and off South America. Unlike privateers, buccaneers had no official government commission, but still attacked only their country's enemies.

Buddhism
An Indian religion established around 500 B.C. by Siddhartha Gautama that preaches the progressive purification of the soul by the renunciation of all worldly concerns.

bullion
Gold and silver ingots.

Burgundy
A duchy in what is now east–central France that became very powerful in the 15th century under a series of strong dukes.

Burma, Kingdom of
State founded by King Anawratha at Pagan in 1044 that unified all Burma; it was overthrown by the Mongols in 1287. Burma was later reunified by the Toungou Dynasty from 1539 on.

Byzantine Empire
The successor to the Eastern Roman Empire, with its capital at Constantinople (present-day Istanbul).

caesarian operation
A surgical operation to deliver a baby by cutting into the mother's womb through the abdominal wall, named for the Roman emperor Julius Caesar, who is said to have been delivered in this way.

Calvinist
A follower of the strict Protestant doctrines preached by the reformer John Calvin of Geneva. Calvinists believe that people's fate is divinely preordained at birth.

Cannanore
Port city on the Malabar coast of Kerala in southwestern India. A center of trade with Persia and Arabia from the 12th century, it was settled by the Portuguese and Dutch and later became a key port for the British East India Company.

caravan
A train of pack animals, notably camels, used by merchants to carry goods along such major long-distance routes as the Silk Road to the East and the Salt Route across the Sahara to West Africa.

cartographer
A maker of maps or charts.

Casa de Contratación
Literally "House of Hiring," a body established by Spain's rulers in 1503 to oversee navigation and exploration in the New World. It came to exercise a monopoly of trade with the Americas.

Castile
Former kingdom in northern Spain that derived its name from the large number of castles built on its frontier with the Moors. After its union with Aragon in 1469 the joint realm became the foundation of a united Spain.

Catholic League
Also known as the Dessau League; an alliance of Catholic princes of Germany, formed in 1525 to fight against the Reformation.

Chiangmai
City in northwestern Thailand on the Ping River. Founded in 1296, it became the capital of the united Kingdom of Laos from 1353 on.

Church of England
Independent branch of the Christian church that came into being in 1534 following the English King Henry VIII's break with Rome in order to obtain a divorce from Catherine of Aragon. Elizabeth I confirmed its status as a Protestant episcopalian church (one having bishops).

Cochin
City and region on the Malabar coast of southwestern India. Portuguese settlers founded the first European fort in India there in the 16th century, but it was overrun by the Dutch in 1663.

colonialism
A system by which strong states exercise administrative control over weaker ones, supposedly in the best interests of the colonized states' subjects.

Confucianism
The doctrine derived from the teachings of the celebrated Chinese administrator and philosopher Confucius (551–479 B.C.), known in China as Kongfuzi. In later times Confucianism, which emphasized learning, respect, and good conduct, became a state religion in China.

conquistador
The Spanish word for "conqueror," used of the explorers and adventurers who conquered the native peoples of Central and South America in the early 16th century.

Council of Trent
General council of the Roman Catholic church that met at Trent, a town in the foothills of the Alps between Italy and Austria, in three sessions, from 1545 to 1547, 1551 to 1552, and 1562 to 1563. It redefined Catholic teaching and is regarded as one of the starting points for the Counter Reformation.

Counter Reformation
A reform movement that got underway in the Roman Catholic church from the mid-16th century in response to the challenge presented by the Protestant Reformation.

Crimea
A peninsula in Ukraine extending into the Black Sea.

culverin
A long-barreled early type of cannon.

czar
The title of the ruler of Russia, derived from the Roman imperial title "caesar." It was adopted by Ivan IV the Terrible in 1547 and was used by his successors until the Russian monarchy was abolished in 1917.

daimyo
In Japan local warlords who seized power for themselves during the Onin War (1467–1477). They ruled the surrounding countryside from strongly defended castles and built up personal armies of samurai warriors, whom they rewarded with landed estates.

Dai Viet
Also known as Annam. A state located in what is now northern Vietnam that was conquered in about 214 B.C. by the Chinese, who named it An-Am, "Peaceful South." Independent from 939, Dai Viet was incorporated into Vietnam in 1946.

Dalai Lama
The title bestowed on the spiritual leader of the dominant "Yellow Hat" sect of Buddhist monks in Tibet by the Mongol Emperor Altan Khan in 1577. The fifth Dalai Lama (1617–1682) assumed secular authority and unified Tibet under his rule.

Deccani Sultanates
Group of five Muslim states on the Deccan Plateau of central India: Bijapur, Ahmadnagar, Golconda, Berar, and Bidar. Created from the breakup of the Bahmani Kingdom from 1490 on, they succumbed to Mughal expansion in the 17th century.

Delhi Sultanate
The Muslim kingdom established in northern India by Muhammad Ghuri when he captured Delhi in 1193. Under his successors it would expand to rule much of the subcontinent. Surviving Genghis Khan's invasion of 1222 in a weakened state, the sultanate was finally destroyed by the onslaught of Timur's forces in 1398.

devshirme
The draft of young Christian boys sent from the Balkans each year to the Ottoman court and forcibly converted to Islam.

Diet of Worms
An assembly of the princes of the Holy Roman empire held at the city of Worms in Germany in 1521 in the presence of the Emperor Charles V, at which Martin Luther was invited to withdraw his demands for reform of the Roman Catholic church. On refusing to do so, he was banished, and an edict was issued condemning his writings.

Din-I Ilahi
Literally "divine faith." New religion established by the Mughal Emperor Akbar (reigned 1555–1605) after disputes with orthodox Muslim leaders who criticized his relaxed attitude toward other faiths.

Discalced Carmelites
A branch of the Carmelite religious order of friars and nuns reformed by St. Teresa of Avila and St. John of the Cross, the spiritual leaders of the Spanish Counter Reformation. "Discalced" literally means "barefoot" or "without sandals"; the friars followed a rule of extreme religious austerity.

Diu
Small island off the coast of Gujarat in western India. Captured by Portugal in 1534, it developed into an important trading base.

Dominican Order
An order of friars (wandering monks) founded by St. Dominic (c.1170–1221). Rather than minister to the poor like the Franciscans, their mission was to spread the orthodox Catholic word among pagans, Muslims, and errant Christian sects.

Dutch War of Independence
The war fought by the seven northern provinces of the Spanish Netherlands (the United Provinces) against Spanish rule. The uprising began in 1567; independence was achieved by 1609 but not formally recognized by Spain until 1648.

encomienda
A system of forced labor in Spanish America by which native peoples were made to work lands assigned to individual conquistadors in return for protection and instruction in the Christian faith.

excommunication
A judgment issued by the pope or a bishop banning an individual from participating in the rites of the Catholic church for a limited or indefinite period.

Ferghana, Kingdom of
Small realm in Central Asia ruled in the 15th century by the descendants of Timur (the Timurids). In the early 16th century the Uzbeks incorporated it into the nearby Khanate of Kokand. Babur, the son of the last ruler of Ferghana, founded the powerful Mughal Dynasty of India.

Franciscan Order
A religious order founded by St. Francis of Assisi (c.1181–1226) whose members were friars living among the people as wandering beggars, rather than monks cloistered in settled monasteries.

Funj
Sultanate in what is now Sudan, founded by Amara Dunkas in 1504. It came to dominate the trans-Saharan trade in gold.

Gakhars
Warrior tribe of northwest India and Pakistan that remained loyal to the Mughal Emperor Humayun when he was deposed by Sher Shah Sur in 1539.

Genoa
An important seaport and center of commerce on the northwest coast of Italy that competed with Venice for Mediterranean trade in the 15th century.

Goa
Port city in west–central India bordering the Arabian Sea. The city of Old Goa, founded by Afonso de Albuquerque in 1510, became the capital of Portuguese India.

Golconda
City and state on the Deccan Plateau of central India that from 1518 was one of the five Muslim Deccani Sultanates. It was conquered by the Mughals under Aurangzeb in 1687.

Golden Horde
Also known as the Kipchak Khanate. Western portion of the Mongol Empire, covering most of Russia. It was founded in the mid-13th century by Genghis Khan's grandson Batu.

Gonds
Aboriginal Dravidian people of eastern India, who inhabited the region known as Gondwana. The Gonds formed several kingdoms between the 12th and 18th centuries before the region came under the sway first of the Marathas and then the British.

Gregorian calendar
The calendar introduced by Pope Gregory XIII in 1582, still in use today, to correct errors in the Julian calendar it replaced. Mistakes had arisen because the average Julian year of 365 and a quarter days was 11 minutes and 10 seconds longer than the solar year.

Guinea Company
The company licensed by Portugal in the 1480s to exploit the resources of Guinea and West Africa, particularly the trade in slaves bound for Brazil. In 1588 the English licensed their own Guinea Company.

Gujarat
Region of west–central India around the city of Goa. An expanding independent Muslim state from 1401, it was annexed by the Mughals in 1574.

guru
A Hindu, Buddhist, or Sikh spiritual leader. In Sikhism the term is specifically applied to the religion's ten founding patriarchs.

Hapsburg Dynasty
Rulers of Austria from 1278 until 1918, who held the title of Holy Roman emperor in an unbroken line from 1438 until 1806. In the 16th and 17th centuries a branch of the Hapsburg family provided the rulers of the Spanish Empire.

harquebus
An early type of portable gun supported on a tripod or on a forked rest that was braced against the shoulder. Sometimes spelled "arquebus."

Hausa
A people living in scattered communities along West Africa's Niger River, which came together to form larger states around 1200. The Hausa Confederation was incorporated into the Songhay Empire from 1512 to 1517.

Hinduism
The dominant religion and culture of India since ancient times. A complex system of beliefs and customs, it includes the worship of many gods and a belief in rebirth.

Hispanic
Of Spanish culture or origin.

Hispaniola
Large Caribbean island, now divided between the states of Haiti and the Dominican Republic. In the 16th century it was the center of Spanish colonial power in the region.

Holy League
An alliance organized in 1511 by Pope Julius II to drive the armies of France out of northern Italy. It included Spain, Venice, the Holy Roman Empire, and England.

Holy Roman emperor
A title bestowed by the pope on a leading central European ruler, thought of as the chief secular champion of the Christian cause. The first Holy Roman emperor was the Frankish Emperor Charlemagne, crowned in 800; the title was finally abolished by Napoleon Bonaparte in 1806.

Huguenots
French Protestants of the 16th and 17th centuries. The derivation of the name is uncertain.

humanist
A person embracing humanism, a worldview popularized during the Renaissance that made human beings rather than God the focus of intellectual attention.

Hussite Wars
Religious wars that set followers of the Bohemian (Czech) church reformer Jan Hus, burned at the stake for heresy in 1415, against the forces of the Holy Roman emperors and the Catholic church. The Hussites were Bohemian nationalists, equally hostile to secular and ecclesiastical authorities.

Imperial City
Palace complex in the Chinese capital of Beijing, constructed from 1406 to 1421. The seat of the Ming (and later the Qing) Dynasty, it took the form of an extensive walled enclosure surrounding the Forbidden City.

Inca
Name of the dynasty that ruled an empire centered on Cuzco in southern Peru in the 15th century. The term also served as the title of the ruling emperor and has since been applied to his subject peoples.

indulgence
Paper granting absolution for sins, thereby shortening the time a sinner spent in purgatory. The sale of indulgences by representatives of the medieval Catholic church was one of the abuses most criticized by Protestant reformers.

Inquisition
Roman Catholic court established in 1233 to suppress heresy. At first punishment was by excommunication; later fines, imprisonment, torture, and execution were used.

Islam
Literally "surrender" to God's will, the faith based on the teachings of the Prophet Muhammad in 7th-century Arabia and subsequently spread by military expansion and trade through much of West Asia and beyond. Its followers are known as Muslims.

Jaga
The name collectively applied to bands of raiders who, in the drought-destabilized decades of the late 16th century, entered Angola and Kongo from the east, attacking and plundering settled communities.

Jainism
A religion founded in India by the 6th century B.C.. Jainism teaches the necessity of self-denial in order to obtain liberation of the soul and urges sympathy and compassion for all forms of life.

janissaries
The personal bodyguard of the Ottoman Sultan (from the Turkish *yeniçeri*, meaning "new force"), recruited from the Christian boys drafted to the sultan's court under the devshirme system.

Jesuit
A member of the Society of Jesus.

jiziya
A tax levied by Islamic rulers on non-Muslim inhabitants of conquered lands.

Julian calendar
A calendar introduced in 45 B.C. by Julius Caesar. It had 12 months rather than the previous ten; the additional months, July and August, were named for the emperors Caesar and Augustus.

Kaaba
A small, cubic temple of bricks draped in black silk housing a sacred stone (presumably a meteorite) that fell from the heavens in ancient times. Built according to tradition by Ibrahim (Abraham) and his son Ishmael in Mecca, the Kaaba is the central shrine of Islam.

Kandy, Kingdom of
Independent monarchy in Sri Lanka that emerged at the end of the 15th century. After withstanding incursions by the Portuguese and Dutch, it was the last Sinhalese kingdom to fall to a colonial power when conquered by the British in 1818.

Kanem-Bornu, Kingdom of
The central African state of Kanem was originally established in about 800 A.D., and by the 11th century it had become a major trans-Saharan trading center. From the late 14th century on its capital was moved to the Bornu region, west of Lake Chad, and the kingdom was subsequently generally referred to as Kanem–Bornu.

kanpaku
Japanese term denoting a regent acting for an emperor who was no longer a minor.

Kashgar
Key trading center in Central Asia on the major caravan routes into the Ferghana Valley. Originally under Chinese control, it fell to the Mongols in 1219, was sacked by Timur the Lame in the late 14th century, and came under the rule of the Chinese Qing Dynasty from 1755 onward.

Kazan, Khanate of
A region on the middle Volga River in Central Asia that was part of the empire of the Golden Horde until its conquest by Ivan IV of Russia in 1552.

Kerala
Southwestern region of India, bordering the Malabar coast of the Arabian Sea, that came under Portuguese rule as a center of the spice trade.

khanate
The name given to a realm ruled by a khan, the title taken by the Mongol conqueror Genghis and his successors on assuming power. The word also eventually came to be used by non-Mongol rulers in China, Central Asia, and Turkey.

Khmers
People of Southeast Asia centered in Cambodia and Laos. The Khmer Empire reached its height in the 10th to 12th centuries, when its capital was Angkor; abandoned in the 15th century under Siamese pressure, the site fell into ruin.

Khurasan
Region of central Iran that in medieval times was often invaded by nomadic peoples from Central Asia. Conquered by Genghis Khan's Mongols and then the forces of Timur the Lame, Khurasan was later incorporated into the Persian Safavid Empire.

Kilwa
Situated on a small island off what is now Tanzania, this port was for many centuries one of the main trading centers of East Africa's Swahili Coast, but it suffered badly at the hands of Portuguese raiders in the 16th century.

Knights Hospitallers
Members of a religious military order established to defend the Latin Kingdom of Jerusalem in the 12th century.

Kongo, Kingdom of
Bantu-speaking kingdom south of the Congo River in central Africa. It survived until 1665, when it broke up following military defeat at the hands of the Portuguese.

Kotte, Kingdom of
Sinhalese kingdom based in southwestern Sri Lanka. At its height in the 15th century it briefly unified all the island, but was weakened by the separation of Jafna and Kandy in 1477 and was subjugated by the Portuguese in the 16th century.

Labrador
A coastal area of what is now eastern Canada, between Hudson Bay and the St. Lawrence River.

Laos, Kingdom of
Buddhist kingdom founded in the mid-14th century; later based at Chiangmai, it reached its zenith under King Souligna Vongsa (r. 1637–1694), but split into three rival kingdoms (Vientiane, Luang Prabang, and Champasak) amid dynastic feuds from 1707 onward.

Laws of the Indies
Generally, the body of laws by which the Spanish crown governed its colonies in the Americas. More specifically, the term is applied to the New Laws passed in 1542 to bring the colonies more closely under royal control, often seen as bringing the conquistador era to an end.

League of Cambrai
A military alliance, named for the town in northern France where its terms were agreed, made between the pope, the Holy Roman emperor, and the kings of France and Aragon in 1508 to put a stop to the territorial ambitions of Venice. League commitments led to France's growing involvement in the wars of northern Italy.

Livonia
A region on the east coast of the Baltic Sea, equivalent to most of present-day Latvia and Estonia, which was ruled by the crusading order of Teutonic Knights from the 13th to the 16th century, when it was divided between Poland and Sweden after the Livonian War with Russia (1558–1582).

Lutheranism
Branch of Protestantism that follows the teachings and principles of the German theologian Martin Luther (1483–1546).

Macao
Port in southern China on the Pearl River estuary. Settled by the Portuguese in 1557, it became a key trade and missionary base; persecuted Japanese Christians sheltered there after the failed Shimabara rebellion (1637). Sovereignty over Macao reverted to China in 1999.

Mahabharata
Indian epic poem describing the dynastic power struggles of a line of Aryan rulers in northern India, possibly in the 10th century B.C.

Majapahit
A Hindu kingdom based on the island of Java that was established in the late 13th century and embarked on an aggressive campaign of expansion in the mid-14th. By the 1360s the Majapahit Empire included most of modern Indonesia and Malaya.

Mamelukes
Originally descended from freed Turkic slaves, the Mamelukes were a military elite who seized power in Egypt in 1250, establishing a dynasty that lasted until 1517.

Mannerism
A style of 16th-century art and architecture (c.1530–1590) that was characterized by unusual effects of scale, light, and perspective, the contortion of natural forms, and the use of bright, harsh colors.

matchlock
An early mechanism for firing a gun. It consisted of a lighted wick (the match) fixed to a pivoting arm, which was lowered into the flashpan to ignite the powder-charge when the marksman depressed the trigger. Also the name for the gun itself.

mausoleum
An elaborate building designed to house the tomb of a famous individual.

Maya
Amerindian people of the Yucatán Peninsula and adjoining areas of southern Mexico, Guatemala, and Honduras. The Maya of the Classic Period (c.250–800 A.D.) are noted for their stepped pyramids, carved monuments, and knowledge of astronomy. They used a pictographic form of writing.

Mecca
The city in western Arabia where the Prophet Muhammad was born in the 6th century A.D., but sacred long before that time thanks to the presence of the sacred stone known as the Kaaba.

Milan, Duchy of
A city and surrounding region of Lombardy in northern Italy that became an independent duchy in the 14th century. Milan was ruled by the Visconti and Sforza families until 1535, when it passed to the Spanish crown.

Ming Dynasty
The last indigenous Chinese dynasty, founded by Zhu Yuanzhang, who reconquered China from the Mongol Yuan Dynasty in 1368. It was finally supplanted by the Manchu (Qing) dynasty in 1644.

missionary
Someone who undertakes the task of spreading the Christian religion to unconverted peoples.

Mon Dynasty
Rulers of Lower Burma around the Irrawaddy Delta, the Mons founded the city of Pegu. Conquered by Pagan in the 11th century, they revived to rule until 1539, when they were overrun by the Toungou, whom they eventually reconquered in 1752, only to lose their independence soon after.

Mongols
A loose association of tribal groups of nomadic herdsmen and raiders originating in the steppes of eastern Siberia. Under Ghenghis Khan and his successors they created the largest land empire ever seen.

Moriscos
After the fall in 1492 of Granada, the last Muslim stronghold in Spain, the name given to Spanish Muslims who chose Christian baptism rather than exile and to their descendants.

mosque
From the Arabic *masjid*, "place of prostration," the name given to a Muslim place of worship.

Mughal Dynasty
Dynasty founded by the Mughals, Islamic successors of Timur the Lame, who conquered northern India in 1526 and subsequently extended their rule over much of the subcontinent.

Muhammad
The Prophet of Islam, born in about 570 A.D. in Arabia. By Muslim tradition the words of Allah (God) were dictated to him by the Angel Gabriel in a series of shuras or chapters, later collected into a holy book, the Koran.

Muscat
A seaport on the Gulf of Oman in the far southeast of the Arabian Peninsula that was hotly fought over by Portuguese and Ottoman forces through the 16th century.

Muscovy
State centered on Moscow in western Russia and first established in the 13th century. After the Mongol and Ottoman conquests it became an isolated bulwark of Christianity, following the Orthodox branch of the faith.

Mwene Mutapa
This northern Shona kingdom came to prominence after the collapse of Great Zimbabwe in the 15th century. By 1500 it had conquered the states of Uteve and Mandanda and made itself the main regional power.

Nakaya Dynasty
South Indian dynasty that came into being when provincial governors of the moribund Vijayanagar Empire broke away from their former masters in the 1530s.

Naples, Kingdom of
Medieval kingdom that, with Sicily, came under Spanish control after 1503.

Ndongo, Kingdom of
The rulers of this state south of the Congo River in Africa bore the title *ngola*, from which the Portuguese took the name "Angola." Portugal failed to take Ndongo in the 16th century, but persistent slave raids by its northerly neighbor Kongo steadily eroded the kingdom's strength.

New Albion
Coastal region of California or Oregon visited in 1579 by the English explorer Sir Francis Drake, who claimed it for Britain.

New Spain
The name given to the northern part of Spain's colonial empire on the American mainland. Founded by Hernán Cortés following the conquest of the Aztecs, it eventually stretched north into what is now the southern United States and south to Honduras and El Salvador.

New World
The Western Hemisphere, especially the continental landmasses of North and South America. The term was first used in the 16th century to distinguish the newly discovered lands of Europe's age of exploration from the "Old World" of Europe and Asia.

Northwest Passage
Sea passage from the Atlantic to the Pacific Ocean around the north coast of Canada, long sought unsuccessfully by explorers until finally traversed by the Norwegian Roald Amundsen from 1903 to 1906.

Orthodox church
Also known as the Eastern Orthodox church. The branch of the Christian church recognized throughout the Greek-speaking world of the eastern Mediterranean. Its spiritual head was, and is, the patriarch (archbishop) of Constantinople. The Slavs of eastern Europe and the Russians subsequently became part of the Orthodox church.

Ottoman Empire
Named for Uthman, a Turkic tribal leader who came to prominence in eastern Asia Minor in 1281, the rulers of the Ottoman Dynasty built a great and enduring empire in western Asia and the eastern Mediterranean from the 14th century on.

papacy
The ruling body of the Catholic church, headed by the pope (the bishop of Rome).

papal bull
An edict issued by the pope (from the Latin *bulla*, meaning "seal").

Peace of Augsburg
The religious settlement that in 1555 established the right of the princes of the Holy Roman Empire, rather than the emperor, to decide the religion of their subjects.

Pegu
City in southern Burma, founded in 825 A.D. as the capital of the Mon kingdom and later ruled by the Toungou until the restoration of the Mons in the 1750s.

Plato
Greek philosopher (c.428–347 B.C.) who founded his own school of philosophy, the Academy, in Athens. He was a follower of Socrates and wrote an account of Socrates's trial. His best known work, *The Republic*, outlines his vision of the ideal state.

Popol Vuh
Mythological work of the Quiché Maya people, describing events before the creation of the human race. It is considered the most substantial piece of Mesoamerican literature to have survived the Spanish conquest.

Protestant
Any of the churches or their members that broke with the Roman Catholic church in the course of the Reformation. Protestants originally took their name from the "Protestation" by supporters of Martin Luther against the decision made at the Diet of Speyer in 1529 to reaffirm the edict of the Diet of Worms against Luther's teachings.

Punjab
One of the northernmost districts of India, bordering what is now Pakistan, and the first area to fall before the advance of Mahmud of Ghazni's Islamic forces in the 11th century.

Puritan
A Christian of strict Protestant persuasion who opposed the role of bishops in the church hierarchy and sought a simple and plain form of worship.

Quiché Maya
A Maya people who inhabited the midwestern highlands of Guatemala; accounts of their history and mythology are preserved in the *Popul Vuh*, written down in the Quiché language using the Latin alphabet in the decades following the Spanish conquest in 1524.

Rajasthan
Region of northwest India, originally known as Rajputana; ruled by the Rajputs until its conquest by the Mughals in the 16th century.

Rajputs
Hindu landowning class of northwest India (Rajputana, later Rajasthan). Rising to prominence from the 9th century and reaching their height in the early 16th, they ruled such cities as Jodhpur and Jaipur. Akbar allowed them independence within the Mughal Empire, and they subsequently ruled as autonomous princes under the British Raj.

recantation
The withdrawal of a former belief or opinion, usually with a public confession of error.

Reformation
The 16th-century religious movement that began with the demand by Luther, Zwingli, and others for the reform of abuses within the Roman Catholic church. The Reformation led to the founding of the Protestant churches and the political division of Europe along religious lines.

regent
A person who governs a kingdom or other domain in place of the sovereign, who may be too young to rule, absent, or incapacitated (for instance, by mental illness).

Renaissance
A revival of classical (Greek and Latin) learning that started in Italy in the 14th century and eventually spread across Europe. The intellectual ferment stimulated a great age of creativity and innovation in the arts.

Rozwi Empire
The state created by the Rozwi, a dynasty of Shona chiefs that emerged in the southwest of the Zimbabwe Plateau in the late 16th century. They grew wealthy by exacting tribute from merchants trading across their territories.

Saadi Dynasty
A line of Arab rulers who originated in Arabia but eventually came to prominence in Morocco. Taking Marrakesh in 1525 and Fez in 1550, they made Morocco prosperous, maintaining diplomatic and trading relations with both the Islamic and Christian worlds.

Safavid Dynasty
Beginning with Esmail I in 1501, this Persian dynasty came to rule over not only Iran but also Armenia, Georgia, and parts of Uzbekistan, Turkmenistan, Azerbaijan, and Afghanistan. Esmail's support for the Shiite branch of Islam had a profound impact on the region's subsequent history.

St. Bartholomew's Day Massacre
The bloodiest event of the French Wars of Religion, when in 1572 Catholics slaughtered thousands of French Protestants.

schism
A split in a body such as a church, usually caused when a group breaks away owing to differences of belief or practice.

Schmalkaldic League
A defensive alliance formed by a number of Protestant princes and cities of the Holy Roman Empire in 1531 to defend themselves from attack by the Emperor Charles V. It was named for the town of Schmalkalden in Germany.

Scholasticism
The rigid system of teaching in the medieval "schools" or universities of western Europe, which held that all philosophical speculation should be directed to a better understanding of Christian theology.

Sennar
This city by the Blue Nile was the capital of the Funj Sultanate, which is consequently sometimes known as the Kingdom of Sennar.

shah
The title assumed by the rulers of Persia

Sharifian Dynasty
An alternative name for Morocco's Saadi Dynasty and its successor, drawing on the fact that their rulers claimed descent from Muhammad through the Prophet's daughter Fatima. (Such descendants are known by the Arabic word *sharif*, "illustrious one.") The Saadi Dynasty is correctly the First Sharifian Dynasty. Quarrels within the family led to the replacement of the Saadi by the Second Sharifian or Alawi Dynasty, which took over in 1660 and rules to this day.

Sher Shah Sur
Also called Sher Khan (c.1486–1545). Afghan emperor of northern India who, after serving the first Mughal ruler Babur, seized power from his successor Humayun, proclaiming himself ruler of Delhi in 1540. His administrative reforms were adopted and extended by Akbar the Great.

Shiites
Muslims of the Shia-i Ali, the "Party of Ali," claiming allegiance to Muhammad's son-in-law and to those imams believed to be his spiritual successors.

shogun
Literally "commander of the imperial guard," the title given from 1192 on to the leader of Japan's ruling warrior family. For almost seven centuries the shoguns were the true rulers of Japan, leaving the country's emperors to occupy themselves primarily with ceremonial duties.

Shona
A collection of communities dwelling in the grasslands of southeast Africa and united by both language and a pastoralist (herding) lifestyle. A succession of Shona states grew rich and powerful by exploiting the region's gold and ivory.

Sikhism
A religion founded in the Punjab in northwestern India by Nanak (1469–1539). Sikhs believe in a single God who is the immortal creator of the universe and in the equality of all human beings.

Silk Road
Ancient overland trade routes extending for roughly 4,000 miles (6,400 km) between China and Europe.

Sinan
The greatest architect of the Ottoman era. Born to Greek Christian parents in 1489, Sinan was taken in boyhood as a janissary or slave soldier of the sultan. He showed a flair for military engineering and then for architecture; by 1539 he was the official architect of Suleiman I.

Sistine Chapel
A chapel in the Vatican built in the late 15th century by Pope Sixtus IV; its many Renaissance artworks include a painted ceiling and fresco of the Last Judgment by Michelangelo.

Sitavaka, Kingdom of
State in southwestern Sri Lanka that arose c.1521 after the decline of the Kingdom of Kotte. Its rulers struggled in vain to expel the Portuguese from the island; the ruling dynasty came to an end in 1594.

Society of Jesus
A religious order of priests founded by the Spanish mystic and former soldier Ignatius Loyola (1491–1556) to fight heresy. It played an important part in the Counter Reformation.

Songhai Empire
A trading empire centered on the city of Gao in what is now northwestern Nigeria. It emerged to eclipse Mali in the 15th century.

Spice Islands
Former name of the Molucca archipelago of eastern Indonesia, famous for the production of spices, especially nutmeg, mace, and cloves.

Stockholm Bloodbath
The mass execution of Swedish nobles in 1520 by Danish forces under King Christian II. The massacre had the effect of hardening Swedish resistance to the Union of Kalmar.

supernova
A giant star that suddenly increases very greatly in brightness because of an explosion ejecting most of its mass.

Swahili
Deriving from the Arabic *sahil* or "coast," Swahili is the language still spoken down much of Africa's eastern seaboard. It is a Bantu-based tongue into which innumerable Arabic words have been absorbed through centuries of commercial and cultural contact.

synod
A church council or ecclesiastical court.

Taklamakan Desert
Extensive arid region of Central Asia occupying the greater part of the Tarim Basin between the Tien Shan and Kunlun mountain ranges. It was home to the khanates of Turfan and Kashgar after c.1500.

Tatars
The name given to the peoples of the Golden Horde, descendants of mixed Turkic–Mongolian ancestry of the Mongol army of Genghis Khan that conquered much of Russia in the 13th century. The Russians continued to pay large amounts of tribute to the Golden Horde until 1480.

tea ceremony
An important household ritual in Japan in which tea prepared in special utensils is offered to guests in a set order. Tea drinking was introduced to Japan by Zen monks, who drank it to keep awake while meditating. The tea ceremony later spread outside the monasteries, becoming an occasion for friends to gather and discuss aesthetics.

Ternate
Small island in the western Moluccas that was the seat of an independent Muslim sultanate and a source of spices, fruit, and coffee for Portuguese traders, who first visited it in 1521. An alliance against the Portuguese between the sultan and the Dutch in the late 16th century ended with the Dutch takeover of Ternate early in the 17th.

Teutonic Knights
Members of a German Christian military order founded in 1190 in Palestine, who wore white robes with black crosses. From 1228 they conducted crusades against the pagan Prussians and Balts of northeastern Europe, subsequently controlling Prussia until the 16th century.

Toungou Dynasty
Dynasty that unified Burma from 1539 on after the capture of the Mon capital Pegu. Its greatest rulers, Tabinshweti and Bayinnaung, subdued the Shans as well as the Mons. The realm lost ground to neighboring powers in the 17th century when Burma fragmented into a multitude of smaller states.

Treaty of Amasya
An agreement in 1555 between Ottoman Turkey and Safavid Iran that recognized Ottoman suzerainty over Iraq. By ending mutual hostilities between the two powers, it enabled both to attain their full magnificence.

Treaty of Cateau-Cambrésis
The treaty between France and Spain that in 1559 recognized Italy as an area of Spanish influence.

Treaty of Granada
A treaty signed in 1500 between King Louis XII of France and the Spanish monarch Ferdinand II of Aragon in which the two powers agree to divide the Kingdom of Naples between them.

Treaty of Saragossa
Agreement made in 1529 between Spain and Portugal to revise the Treaty of Tordesillas—which in 1494 had drawn the boundaries between the overseas conquests of the countries—in favor of Spain.

Treaty of Tordesillas
Treaty made between Spain and Portugal in 1494 to resolve disputes over the two nations' rival claims to newly discovered lands in the Americas. The treaty proposed a line 370 leagues (1,150 miles) west of Cape Verde; all lands to the west of it were to belong to Spain, all to the east to Portugal.

Tumed Mongols
Branch of the Khalka Mongols inhabiting eastern Mongolia. Under their leader Altan Khan (1507–1582) they became dominant over the western Oirat Mongols and captured the former Great Khanate capital at Karakorum; Tumed influence declined after Altan Khan's death.

Union of Kalmar
The union of Denmark, Sweden, and Norway under one crown, formed in 1397. Swedish nobles came to resent having a king residing in Copenhagen, Denmark, and broke away several times. Finally, in 1523 Gustav I Vasa, a Swedish nobleman, led a successful uprising against Denmark and was elected king of Sweden, thus ending the union.

Union of Lublin
The union of Poland with the Grand Duchy of Lithuania that in 1569 created a single kingdom headed by a king jointly elected by the nobles of Poland and Lithuania.

Union of Utrecht
Defensive alliance of the seven northern provinces of the Netherlands against Spain. The union became the foundation of the Dutch Republic.

usurper
Someone who seizes a kingdom or political power unlawfully.

Uzbeks
Nomadic pastoralists (herders) of Turkic origin inhabiting the steppes of Central Asia, in particular the area now known as Uzbekistan. In the 16th century their raids represented a real threat to the rising power of Safavid Persia.

Vatican
The palace and official residence of the pope in Rome.

Venice, Republic of
An independent republic ruled by a doge or chief magistrate from the port of Venice on the Adriatic coast of northeast Italy. A major sea power from the 13th to the 16th century through its control of trade with West Asia, Venice ruled islands and ports in the eastern Mediterranean as well as part of the Italian mainland (the Veneto).

viceroy
Literally "vice (or deputy) king," a viceroy rules a province or conquered territory on behalf of his sovereign.

Vijayanagar
Powerful Hindu kingdom of southern India that flourished from the mid-14th to the 16th century.

vizier
The chief minister of the Seljuk Empire; used loosely, the term was later applied to the chief administrative official in many Muslim countries.

wheel lock
A later refinement of the matchlock that substituted a flint and spring-loaded wheel for the lighted wick. When the trigger was pulled, the flint struck the wheel to make a spark that ignited the powder charge.

White Sheep Turkmen
A federation of Turkmen tribes in eastern Anatolia, northern Iraq, and western Iran, formed in the 14th century in rivalry with the Black Sheep Turkmen farther south. It was forced into retreat by the expansion of Safavid Persia in the 16th century.

Xavier, St. Francis
Spanish Jesuit missionary who introduced Christianity to India (Goa) from 1542 to 1545 and to Japan from 1548 to 1551, when he visited the then-capital Kyoto and Kagoshima.

Xhosa
A predominantly pastoralist (herding) people living in the southeast of what is now South Africa. At the start of the 16th century they were comparative newcomers, having migrated into the region from the north not long before.

Zeydis
A breakaway sect of Shiite Muslims for whom the succession of sacred teachers, or imams, should have come down through Zeyd ibn Ali, great grandson of Ali, Muhammad's cousin, whom Shiites see as Muhammad's spiritual heir.

FURTHER READING

Bainton, Roland H. *Here I Stand: A Life of Martin Luther*. Nashville, TN: Abingdon Press, 1990.

Berinstain, Valerie. *India and the Mughal Dynasty*. New York, NY: Abrams, 1998.

Black, C.F., et al. *Cultural Atlas of the Renaissance*. New York, NY: Prentice Hall General Reference, 1993.

Black, Jeremy. *War and the World: Military Power and the Fate of Continents 1450–2000*. New Haven, CT: Yale University Press, 1998.

Boxer, C.R. *The Portuguese Seaborne Empire 1415–1825*. New York, NY: A.A. Knopf, 1969.

Clot, André. *Suleiman the Magnificent: The Man, His Life, His Epoch*. London, UK: Saqi Books, 1992.

Connah, Graham. *African Civilizations: An Archaeological Perspective*. New York, NY: Cambridge University Press, 2nd edn., 2001.

De Madariaga, Isabel. *Ivan the Terrible*. New Haven, CT: Yale University Press, 2005.

Dickens, A.G. *Reformation and Society in 16th-century Europe*. New York, NY: Harcourt, Brace, and World, 1966.

Elton, G.R.. *Reformation Europe 1517–1559*. Malden, MA: Blackwell Publishers, 1999.

Elton, G.R. *England under the Tudors*. New York, NY: Routledge, 3rd edn., 1991.

Fennell, J.L.I. ed. *Prince A.M. Kurbsky's History of Ivan IV*. Cambridge, UK: Cambridge University Press, 1965.

Gascoigne, Bamber. *A Brief History of the Great Moghuls*. London, UK: Robinson, 2002.

Goodwin, Jason. *Lords of the Horizons: A History of the Ottoman Empire*. New York, NY: H. Holt, 1999.

Guy, John. *Tudor England*. New York, NY: Oxford University Press, reprint edn., 1990.

Hall, Bert. S. *Weapons and Warfare in Renaissance Europe: Gunpowder, Technology, and Tactics*. Baltimore, MD: John Hopkins University Press, 2002.

Hay, Denys. *The Italian Renaissance in Its Historical Background*. New York, NY: Cambridge University Press, 2nd edn., 1977.

Hemming, John. *The Conquest of the Incas*. New York, NY: Harvest/HBJ Books, 2003.

Inalcik, Halil. *The Ottoman Empire: The Classical Age 1300–1600*. London, UK: Phoenix Press, 2000.

Janelle, Pierre. *The Catholic Reformation*. Milwaukee, WI: Bruce Publishing Co., 1963.

MacCulloch, Diarmaid. *The Reformation: A History*. New York, NY: Modern Library, 2004.

Martin, Colin, and Geoffrey Parker. *The Spanish Armada*. New York, NY: St. Martin's Press, revised edn., 2002.

Mattingly, Garrett. *The Defeat of the Spanish Armada*. Boston, MA: Houghton Mifflin, 1984.

Morison, Samuel Eliot. *The European Discovery of America: The Southern Voyages A.D. 1492–1616*. New York, NY: Oxford University Press, 1974.

Parker, Geoffrey. *Philip II*. Chicago, IL: Open Court, 1995.

Parker, Geoffrey. *The Military Revolution: Military Innovation and the Rise of the West 1500–1800*. New York, NY: Cambridge University Press, 2nd edn., 1996.

Parry, J.H. *The Spanish Seaborne Empire*. Berkeley, CA: University of California Press, reprint edn., 1990.

Payne, Robert. *Ivan the Terrible*. New York, NY: Cooper Square Press, 2002.

Richards, John F. *The Mughal Empire*. New York, NY: Cambridge University Press, new edn., 1996.

Somerset, Anne. *Elizabeth I*. New York, NY: Anchor Books, 2003.

Thackston, W.M., Jr., ed. *The Baburnama: Memoirs of Babur, Prince and Emperor*. New York, NY: Modern Library, 2002.

Vogel, Joseph O. *Great Zimbabwe: The Iron Age in South Central Africa*. New York, NY: Garland Publishing, 1994.

Wachtal, Nathan. *The Vision of the Vanquished: The Spanish Conquest of Peru through Indian Eyes, 1530–1570*. New York, NY: Barnes and Noble, 1977.

White, Jon Manchip. *Cortés and the Downfall of the Aztec Empire*. New York, NY: Carroll & Graf Publishers, 2nd edn., 1996.

SET INDEX

61